Persuasive Writing & Speaking

Communication Fundamentals for Business

PHYLLIS WACHOB

Nanyang Business School
Nanyang Technological University

Australia • Canada • Mexico • Singapore • Spain • United Kingdom • United States

Persuasive Writing & Speaking: Communication Fundamentals for Business
by Phyllis Wachob

Copyright © 2005 by Thomson Learning (a division of Thomson Asia Pte Ltd).
Thomson Learning™ is a trademark used herein under license.

For more information, please contact:
Thomson Learning
(a division of Thomson Asia Pte Ltd)
5 Shenton Way
#01-01 UIC Building
Singapore 068808

Or visit our Internet site at *http://www.thomsonlearningasia.com*

ALL RIGHTS RESERVED
No part of this work covered by the copyright hereon may be reproduced or used in any form or by any means — graphic, electronic, or mechanical, including photocopying, recording, taping, web distribution or information storage and retrieval systems — without the written permission of the publisher.

For permission to use material from this product, contact us on:
Tel: (65) 6410 1200
Fax: (65) 6410 1208
Email: tlsg.info@thomson.com

Thomson Learning offices in Asia: Bangkok, Beijing, Hong Kong, Kuala Lumpur, Manila, Mumbai, Seoul, Singapore, Taipei, Tokyo.

Printed in Singapore
1 2 3 4 5 6 SLP 07 06 05 04

ISBN 981-254-528-X

contents

Preface	vii
Introduction	1
1 Who Is the Audience?	5
2 What Is the Message?	11
3 Organizing the Message	23
4 Structure and Transitions	37
5 Reasoning	49
6 Supporting the Argument	59
7 Openings and Closings	71
8 Formatting the Message	83
9 Editing and Evaluation	95
10 Putting It All Together	103
Bibliography	111

preface

I decided to write this book when I could not find any other book that had language and topics relevant to the Southeast Asian context and with content related to business. Moreover, most of the other options were not student-friendly; for example, the books were unwieldy. Motivating students with best practice methodologies and lively, appropriate materials is crucial to the success of students in English Proficiency courses.

Students who realize the importance of good English communication skills are able to commit themselves to becoming autonomous learners and continuing their development in the use of the English language.

If I can inspire teachers and students with this slim volume of business-related readings and activities geared toward their local context, then I will have fulfilled my purpose in writing this book for the English Proficiency students of the Nanyang Business School (NBS).

I would like to thank my present and past colleagues who over the years have written material or given me ideas for content. Thanks go to Dr Ho Mian Lian, Dr Arlene Harvey, Dr Michael Connor, Ms Dorothy Lee, Dr Valerie Goby, Dr Lesley Lee, Mr Colin Clark, Ms Catherine Cheng, Dr Justus Lewis, and Dr Irene Wong. I would also like to thank Mr Art Baer of Express Gum and NBS Student Jan Cheo for permission to include material.

Phyllis Wachob

introduction

Why Communication Is Crucial in the Business World

If you can write and speak with confidence, with correct grammar and good organisation, then you will gain credibility with your audience. If you understand the need for choosing the right tone, the proper format, and a concise writing style, then you will succeed in persuading your audience. If you understand the importance of appearance, body language, eye contact, and what constitutes an effective opening and closing to a presentation, then you will have your audience with you. If you fail to do these things, you could lose credibility, lose the deal, not get the job you want, or your fellow employees could turn against you.

Communication is a key element in being a successful business person. Good communicators make it look easy because they have the confidence, the knowledge, and have practiced the skills of good communication.

Teamwork is a crucial part of today's business world. Knowing how to work within a team and to communicate with team members is a vital part of a successful career in business. Learning when to speak, how to listen and give feedback, and how to present an opposite view are some of the skills that require knowledge as well as skill practice.

This book is an introduction to these ideas and gives the beginning business student practice in these skills as well as the basic knowledge of business communication. It is meant as a base on which to build higher-level knowledge and skills. As such, each chapter contains a series of ideas, examples, activities, and questions that can be used as building blocks to greater proficiency.

Chapter Framework

This book is divided into 10 chapters, each focusing on a theme in business communication.

The first chapter starts with the fundamental issue of asking who the audience is and progresses through the other issues that are necessary to craft a communication. The last few chapters deal with editing and finishing the final product.

Within each chapter are five areas of focus. These five areas are meant to give information as well as provide practice in writing and speaking. The main methodology that is suggested to be used with this book is cooperative learning in teams or groups.

 FOCUS ON COMMUNICATION

This section begins every chapter and contains fundamental ideas about communication with specific reference to business communication. This is meant as a background to the activities that follow. The information given will help the student craft the messages that are asked for in the later sections.

 FOCUS ON LANGUAGE

This section focuses on the grammar that is needed to make the writer clearly understood and the message grammatically correct. Explanations are given, some in detail, on selected areas of grammar that are sometimes problematic for Asian students. Teachers should supplement this section with further explanations from grammar textbooks and exercises as needed.

 FOCUS ON WRITING

This segment presents concepts about good written communication in the business context. Letters, memos, emails, and reports are presented with information on different types of organization. Concepts about transition markers, openings and closings, tone, register, and word choice are included. Most of these sections contain an activity that can be used as a portfolio assignment and are marked accordingly.

 FOCUS ON SPEAKING

Speaking clear, understandable English lends credibility to any encounter. This section contains some work on presentation skills and opportunities for group work. Some cooperative writing and language work is done through group speaking activities. Four opportunities for presentations are presented and can be used for diagnostic or assessment purposes.

 FOCUS ON REFLECTION

Confucius said, 'Seeking knowledge without thinking is labor lost; thinking without seeking knowledge is perilous.' We never really learn anything until we think about it.

This section contains a series of discussion questions related to the focus on communication and how it relates to the activities in the chapter. Some time should be given to this section before moving on the next chapter to consolidate concepts, reflect on personal ideas, and review performance in writing and speaking. Only then can students be prepared to tackle the tasks that follow.

How to Use this Textbook

The 10 chapters in this book are designed for a weekly class of 2–4 hours and lasting for a course of 10–12 weeks. Supplemental activities are advised for more language focus or more writing or speaking practice.

Portfolios are an excellent way for students to see their progress and give students and teachers a chance to personalize the writing feedback. One suggestion is to designate certain activities as portfolio assignments and these are marked in the text.

Group work can be used with almost all activities if desired. Students are generally more interested if they can work with their classmates in completing tasks. Review of their work by their peers can give them insight into the skills that they may be lacking. It also gives some students the confidence to consolidate their own knowledge while practicing feedback and listening techniques.

This textbook can be used with any adult-level of learner, but is geared towards college and university-aged students, who perhaps have not had much exposure to the business world yet. Activities are general in nature, but are aimed at the student of business.

chapter 1

Who Is the Audience?

 FOCUS ON COMMUNICATION

No matter what kind of message we send, we must always consider for whom the message is intended. To make our message effective, we must ask the following questions:

1) Who is our audience?
2) What do they already know?
3) What do they think or feel about the subject?

1) Who Is Our Audience?

Sometimes we communicate not just to one audience, but to several. The person or group to whom we directly send our message is the **primary audience**. We may also have a **secondary audience**, comprising a person or group who may hear, read, or discover in other ways, the message we send. This audience may include a boss, other stakeholders in the company, or even a 'hidden' audience.

We must always consider not only the primary audience, but these other audiences who may be gatekeepers or opinion- or decision-makers.

2) What Do They Already Know?

Every communication event needs an **introduction**, but the tone, length, and subject matter may vary depending on what the audience already knows.

We must also consider how much new information is needed in the **body** of the communication. For example, can we assume that all members of the audience are familiar with the situation, the limitations, the jargon, and the outcome? Choosing the right information for the audience can help us decide the style and length of the communication as well.

3) What Do They Think or Feel About the Subject?

Analyzing the biases and emotions of the audience gives us an indication of how to structure our message. Does our target audience have a positive or negative view of the topic? How emotionally involved are they in this message? Is this going to be good news or bad news for them? Good news is an easy message to send, but we must beware of hidden audiences or unstated biases.

Analyzing the audience with regards to what they know and how they are likely to receive the message is the first step towards successful business communication. Every communication must persuade our audience that we are credible, knowledgeable, and care about the recipient.

 FOCUS ON LANGUAGE

ACTIVITY: Taking a Diagnostic Test

In the following memo are 10 grammatical mistakes. Underline the mistakes or indicate by a ^ where something is missing, and then make the correction in the margin. Check with your group to make sure you have corrected all the errors.

> To: Project Managers
> From: Teo Yiling, VP Human Resources
> Date: 25 July 2004
> Subject: Designing a New Letterhead
>
> Nanyang Business Associates (NBA) is sponsoring a contestant among all work teams to design a letterhead for their team. Each team will submit their entry to Larry for judging. All entries will be reviewed by the senior management team, who will decide the winning entry. The winning team gives a lunch at the Jade Dragon Restaurant.
>
> Because keep in mind that your team letterhead will represent NBA. It should be professional, businesslike, and in good taste. Remember, too,

> that letterheads usually took up about 5cm at the top of paper. If possibly, the letterhead should be design on the computer using a word processor or graphics program.
>
> In the future, the project teams would use the letterhead she have designed to submit all project materials to NBA.
>
> The contest deadline are 15 September. Good luck! Have fun!

Adapted from Featheringham and Baker. 2001. *Applications in Business Communication*, p.5.

After your group has found and corrected all the errors, assess your own mistakes. We will be looking closely at all these grammatical mistakes in the weeks to come.

1. Which errors did you not catch?
2. Why?
3. Which ones were easy for you?
4. Which ones were difficult?

As a group, make a list of the most frequent errors that your team mates have made. This is a chance for you to gain awareness of your own and your team mates' language difficulties.

 FOCUS ON SPEAKING

We are frequently asked to introduce ourselves to new friends or colleagues. Having a 'bank of ideas' about ourselves is a useful tool in professional life.

ACTIVITY: Presenting Yourself in an Icebreaker Speech

Think about what you might want to say about yourself to your classmates.

- Who is your audience?
- What do they already know?
- What will they be interested in?

Remember, you want to persuade your class that you are a good person to have as a classmate and team mate. You want to portray yourself honestly, but you also want to establish your credibility.

For five minutes, brainstorm on the things you might tell someone about yourself. Make a list of them, then delete or expand on each item, keeping in mind what you think your classmates would like to hear. Consider also telling an interesting story that reveals something about your personality, ideals, or unique characteristics. Be sure that you have an introduction, a body, and a conclusion.

Introduce yourself to the rest of the class in an oral presentation of 2-3 minutes.

 FOCUS ON WRITING

ACTIVITY: Analyzing the Memo from NBA

Look at the (corrected) memo from the Nanyang Business Associates. Analyze it using the following questions:

1) Who is the primary audience?
2) Who is the secondary audience?
3) What does the audience already know about:
    a) the contest?
    b) the company?
    c) designing letterheads?
4) What do they need to know about the contest?
5) What do you think the audience will think or feel about the contest?

ACTIVITY: Writing a Cover Letter (Portfolio Assignment)

CV is the abbreviation for curriculum vitae, which is a brief account of your qualifications for a job. A cover letter introduces yourself and states why you want to have a job with the company. For this reason, a cover letter needs to be specific for the company or industry you are targeting. It should not contain lists of qualifications that are already in the CV, but information about yourself that would help someone get to know you and think you would be a good person to work for the company.

Using the list of things you made for your oral introduction of yourself, decide if these are things you would want to tell a prospective employer. If not, make a new list. Organize it logically to persuade the reader to continue reading and think about what you have said. Remember, you need to establish your credibility as a potential worker in the company.

Choose a company or an industry where you might want to work. Think of the possible jobs that you might do in a few years' time. Use a real or fictitious name for a company and write a one-page cover letter for your CV.

 FOCUS ON REFLECTION

This chapter has introduced the concept of **audience focus**. In the business world, all communication has an audience and a purpose. This is a fundamental concept that should be incorporated in all communication events.

In the Focus on Language section, we looked at a memo that contained grammatical errors.

1) What could have happened if we had not corrected it before it was sent out?
2) What would the audience think?
3) What misconceptions could they have had about the contest and the prize?
4) Why do we need to use language that is correct and accurate?

In the Focus on Speaking section, we learned to introduce ourselves.

1) Was your presentation interesting?
2) How do you know?
3) What did your audience think?
4) Did you find your classmates' presentations interesting?
5) Why?
6) Do you think differently now that you know something about them?
7) How did you feel when you were introducing yourself?
8) Were you nervous? (Most people are!)
9) What could you do to be more confident?

In the Focus on Writing segment, we started to organize a cover letter to accompany our CV. This is a skill that you can use in the future.

1) When might you want to write a letter of introduction?
2) How did you decide to organize your cover letter?
3) What did it contain?

Reflecting on what we have done and how we did it is a learning strategy that makes it clear to us what we have learned and which areas we need more work in. Professionals in business and education use this strategy to make their work better. It can be used on a daily basis or for a special event. Getting into the habit of reflection can enhance the critical-thinking skills that are needed to be a leader in any field.

1) What kinds of reflection have you done in the past?
2) Has it helped you learn something new?
3) Has it helped you consolidate and revise what you already know?
4) What time of day is good for you to reflect?
5) Have you practiced reflection today?

chapter 2

What Is the Message?

 FOCUS ON COMMUNICATION

After we have decided on who the audience is, we need to decide on what the message will be.

An **informative message** is one that imparts knowledge. Although it may at first appear to be a neutral kind of message, it depends on the audience and how they may react to it. Even in informative messages we need to consider the persuasive aspects of the communication.

Persuasive messages are communications such as recommendations or proposals. **Sensitive messages** are sometimes called 'bad news' messages because they contain potentially negative material. We need to be very persuasive when we write these sensitive messages as we want the readers to remain positive in their attitude towards the sender and the message. This is not an easy task.

There are three different strategies to use in creating a persuasive message depending on the message. **Logos** refers to the use of logic or rational thought to persuade. **Pathos** is the emotional method and **ethos** refers to the credibility of the speaker. If we put ourselves in the position of the recipients and analyze what they may think or feel about the message, we can choose the kind of message we want to send and the best method of persuasion.

ACTIVITY: Analyzing the Kind of Persuasion in a Memo

Look at the memo from the previous chapter (or the text that your teacher provides).

1) Who is the audience?
2) What will persuade them to do as they are asked?
3) Which strategy does the sender choose?
4) Why?

5) What would happen if another persuasive style was chosen?
6) Would it be more or less effective?
7) Why?
8) How can you recognize what kind of persuasive style is used? In the language chosen? In organizational structure?

 FOCUS ON LANGUAGE

Verbs carry meaning in English. They describe action or relationship, tell us about the time when the action took place, indicate who or what did the action, what or to whom the action was done, and convey the mood. This chapter's focus on language will introduce the concept of **time** and **verb tenses**.

There are three main time concepts that we need to take into account: the past, the present, and the future. Also, there is the idea of the simple verb, the progressive aspect, the perfect and the perfect progressive aspect. In this chapter, we will look at six verb tenses and their uses.

Simple Present Tense

The simple present tense is used for more than just describing things that happen in the present. It is also used to indicate a current state, a habitual action, or a general truth:

> Business is an increasingly important activity throughout the world today. (Current state)
>
> Our work starts at nine every morning. (Habitual action)
>
> The early bird gets the worm. (General truth)

Another use of the present tense, especially in literary work such as novels and short stories, is to give immediacy to actions. These actions may have happened in the past, but we want to emphasize the timelessness or the impact on the current state of affairs:

> Confucius tells us that there is a reciprocal relationship between superior and inferior. (Timelessness, as Confucius' words still inform our actions today)

We can also use the simple present tense to refer to actions that we plan to do in the future:

> The product launches in 10 days. (In the future, but the plans have been made)

Present Progressive Tense

This tense indicates an activity in progress or a temporary situation. Like the present tense, it can also be used for a fixed time in the future:

> I am working on the new logo now. (Activity in progress)
>
> Sam is working at the new project headquarters right now. (Temporary situation)
>
> He is returning to the main office in three weeks' time. (Fixed time in the future)

Note that some verbs that refer to mental states or emotions, conditions or relationships are not used in the progressive form. These include believe, belong, contain, cost, know, own, prefer, and want:

> Mary believes that the new office block is better than the old one. (Not 'Mary is believing…')
>
> Leela owns a really good dictionary. (Not 'Leela is owning…')
>
> Mei Fei knows where all the stationery is kept. (Not 'Mei Fei is knowing…')

Simple Past Tense

It describes events or conditions that have happened in the past and are completed:

> Boon Lay Electronics, a family company, was established 40 years ago. (Past action, the establishment is now completed)
>
> The main factory in Malaysia burned down three weeks ago. (Past event)
>
> The police said it was not arson, but they did not say what caused the fire. (Past event)

Present Perfect Tense

This tense combines two time frames: the past and the present. It describes an event in the past; but unlike the simple past tense, the event relates in some way to the present. It can describe an event that started in the past and continues to the present, or a past action that has current relevance. It can also be used to describe an experience that relates to the present context:

> I have worked for Boon Lay Electronics for four years and I have never missed a day's work. (Work started in the past and continues, i.e., never missing work continues)

> I have completed the logo design, so now Jordan can take it to the focus group. (The completion of the logo design is in the past, but the result has relevance to the present)

> I have attended many exhibitions in the new EXPO Center; it is a great place to show off company products. (The experience of attending exhibitions informs the value judgement of the place, which is in the present tense)

Past Perfect Tense

It indicates an action completed in the past before another past action or time:

> He had worked in Nanyang Business Associates for six years before he worked for us. (Two past events, both completed in the past; the one indicated by the past perfect is the first of the two events) Now he works for Boon Lay Electronics.

> By the time he was 23, he had held more than eight different positions in the company owned by his father. (Action completed before a specific past time)

We must be careful not to overuse this verb tense, as most situations of completed past actions are expressed in the past tense.

Past Progressive Tense

The past progressive tense describes repeated or ongoing actions in the past. It is frequently used when there is another action (in the past tense) that interrupts or occurs during the time period:

Sam was talking on the phone when Amit brought him the logo design. (Ongoing action, interrupted by an event in the past)

On Monday morning, the women discussed the projects they were working on. (The point of time is Monday morning, but the period of time is the length of the projects)

ACTIVITY: Finding and Correcting the Errors

In the following press release, there are six verb tense mistakes. Underline them and then in the margin, indicate the correct grammar. Check with your group to make sure you have corrected all the errors.

FOR IMMEDIATE RELEASE

IMPRESS GUM LAUNCHES IN SINGAPORE BECOMING
THE FIRST CHEWING GUM AVAILABLE WITHOUT
A PRESCRIPTION IN MORE THAN 12 YEARS

SANTA BARBARA, California – April 21, 2004 - Impress Gum confirmed the launch of its chewing gum in Singapore today, and has named Kingston Medical Supplies (Pte) Ltd as its exclusive distributor. Impress Gum, which was made in the USA, is the **first chewing gum available in Singapore without a prescription** since the import, manufacture and sale of gum was banned in 1992. Under the US-Singapore Free Trade Agreement (USSFTA), Singapore agreed to allow the importation of chewing gum with therapeutic value. The Heath Sciences Authority, Singapore will grant a product license for Impress Gum to be imported and sold in Singapore.

Impress Gum, a sugar free chewing gum available in Peppermint and Spearmint flavors, is used to freshen breath, whiten teeth and help prevent tooth decay. It will contain Xylitol, a natural sweetener which helps in protecting teeth against dental cavities, and Sodium Bicarbonate which assisted in removing tough stains. Impress Gum has been now available at leading pharmacies and dental clinics throughout Singapore.

"We are very excited to offer our range of chewing gums to the Singapore market," said Art Baer, President and CEO of Impress Gum.

> "We anticipate significant demand in Singapore for Impress Gum," said George Foo, Senior Manager of Kingston Medical Supplies. He had emphasized that "Impress Gum is an excellent adjunct to oral health as it freshens breath, whitens teeth and helps prevent tooth decay, making it a superior product for our consumers. Impress Gum is now available at many of the leading pharmacies and dental clinics throughout Singapore."

After your group has found and corrected all the errors, assess your own mistakes.

1) Which errors did you not catch?
2) Why?
3) Which ones were easy for you?
4) Which ones were difficult?

As a group, make a list of the most frequent errors you and your team mates have made.

FOCUS ON SPEAKING

Brainstorming

Brainstorming is a way to generate ideas. It is best to learn how to brainstorm in a group so that everyone can contribute and think of more ideas. There are two basic ways to brainstorm. The first is to make a simple list of ideas and the second is to draw a mind map, which we will deal with in the next section. If our topic is complex, we can do it both ways. First we make a list, then create a mind map with the ideas and add others as we fill in the map.

Here is an example of a brainstorming session:

Drinks needed for the company picnic
- Coca-Cola
- Mineral water
- Coffee/tea

- Juice
- Sprite
- Soda
- Orange juice
- Jasmine tea
- Newater
- Apple juice
- Soursop juice

Mind Mapping

Below is a simple mind map. Note how the main topic is in the center, subtopics are around it, and items grouped together.

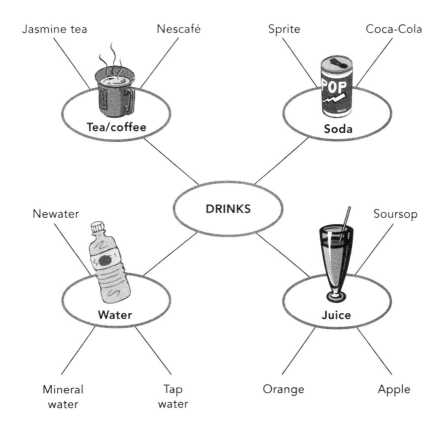

ACTIVITY: Brainstorming

Round 1: Choose a topic from the list of starter topics below or think of something else you want to brainstorm on. Time your group, giving yourselves three minutes to generate ideas. Write them in a **list**. All group members should participate.

Round 2: Choose another topic (maybe one of the ideas from the list you generated in Round 1). Give your group one minute to brainstorm and make a list. Then using the ideas, make a mind map, spending two more minutes expanding on the ideas.

Round 3: Choose a completely different topic. Give your group one minute to make a list and another two minutes to make a mind map.

Brainstorming starter topics:
- Careers in business
- Qualities of a good boss
- Transportation to work/school
- Improvements to working/studying conditions
- Our rival universities
- Topic in the news

 ## FOCUS ON WRITING

ACTIVITY: Peer Reviewing

To be able to see and correct our own mistakes, it is necessary to practice looking closely at grammar. If we start with our peers' work, then it is easier to move on to our own.

1) Exchange papers (your portfolio assignment from Chapter 1) with your team mates.
2) Find and correct any errors you see.
3) Underline all the verbs.
   a) What tense are they in?
   b) Have they been used properly?
   c) If you changed the tense of a verb, would it change the meaning?

Discuss with your team mates the errors that you have found.

ACTIVITY: Discussing Audience Analysis

Read the following extract.

> ### The Target Market
>
> The marketing strategies of determining product, price, placement, and promotion are not planned in isolation. Marketing analysts often look at a combination of these four factors. This combination of the four P's is known as the marketing mix. The elements of the marketing mix focus on the consumer. In order to develop a successful marketing mix, researchers first ask two important questions.
>
> - Who is going to buy the product?
> - What is the potential to sell this product?
>
> The group of customers or consumers who will probably buy the product is known as the target market. The company directs its marketing efforts toward this group of potential customers who form the target market. Once market researchers have determined the target market they wish to appeal to, the company can develop an appropriate mix of product, price, placement, and promotion. The company attempts to match consumer needs or mold consumer desires to the product being offered. For example, if the target market is middle-class teenagers, the marketing mix might consist of the following.
>
> Product: blue jeans
> Price: *with* the average price of the market
> Placement: department store
> Promotion: advertisements on a 'pop music' radio station
>
> A successful marketing mix depends on the knowledge about consumers and their buying habits, gained through market research as well as correct identification of the target market. Strategies of product, price, placement, and promotion are blended in order to reach a chosen group of consumers.

Adapted from Arden and Dowling. 1993. *Business Concepts for English Practice*, p.36.

PERSUASIVE WRITING & SPEAKING

1) Who is the audience for this short reading?
2) What kind of message is it?
3) As a student, do you often read passages such as this?

ACTIVITY: Discussing Market Research and Product Design

Look at the bottle of shampoo below.

1) What information can you get from the label?
2) Who do you think is the target market for this shampoo?
3) Does this shampoo appeal to you?
4) Why or why not?
5) What kinds of messages are being conveyed by the shampoo bottle and its label?
6) What kind of strategies do the senders use?
7) When you buy shampoo, what kind of message from the bottle or advertisement makes you want to buy that particular shampoo?
8) What kinds of messages do advertisers use to sell their products?

ACTIVITY: Conducting a Market Research Survey

In what kinds of stores can you find shampoo?

Choose one store and complete the following market research survey.

(This market research activity will continue for many classes. If you would like to choose another kind of product, such as a soft drink, sports shoes, or some other product that you are familiar with, you may do so. If you choose a different product, alter the market research survey on the next page.)

Market Research Survey

Name of store _____ Location _____

	Brand of shampoo	Price per ml	Color	Slogan
1				
2				
3				
4				
5				

Total number of different brands of shampoo _____

Description or drawing of containers

Target market for each of the five brands of shampoo listed above

1.

2.

3.

4.

5.

Description of the shampoo that appeals to you most

Reasons you like it

Adapted from Arden and Dowling. 1993. *Business Concepts for English Practice*, pp.43–44.

FOCUS ON REFLECTION

This chapter focused on the various kinds of messages we can send to our audience and how we can use different appeals (logos, pathos, and ethos) to achieve our ends.

1) Which kind of persuasive strategy do you think is the most powerful for you?
2) Which kind is most used in advertising?

In the Focus on Language section, we looked at various verb tenses.

1) Have you mastered these verb tenses?
2) Have you learned any strategies that can help you?

In the Focus on Speaking segment, we looked at two ways of brainstorming.

1) Which one appeals to you most?
2) Why?
3) Is it better to brainstorm in a group or by yourself?
4) Why?
5) Do you think it is possible to learn the 'skill' of brainstorming?

In the Focus on Writing section, we were introduced to peer editing.

1) Do you think this is a good idea?
2) What can you learn from peer editing?
3) What can we teach someone else?

chapter 3

Organizing the Message

 FOCUS ON COMMUNICATION

In this chapter, we will look at the ways we can organize our message. After we have decided who our audience is and what kind of message we want to send, we then need to ask ourselves the following:

1) What is the best organization for this message?
2) What do I need to do to make it understandable and convincing?
3) How will my audience read/listen to and understand?

The receiver of a message generally has the highest interest level at the beginning and at the end of a message, and the lowest in the middle. Therefore, **openings** and **closings** are crucial to good communication. This will be covered more thoroughly in Chapter 7.

1) What Is the Best Organization for this Message?

If the message contains good news, this should almost always be stated first. Then the reasons or actions needed to be taken can follow. Sensitive or bad news, however, needs more thought, as do persuasive messages. The body of a message always needs to be logical and understandable.

2) What do I Need to do to Make it Understandable and Convincing?

Messages can be conveyed using different thought processes. The organization of the information depends upon the subject, but there is always more than one way to organize information:

- **Chronology:** Organizing by time sequence
  This method is appropriate when there are many events to report and the sequence of events may be important for understanding.
- **Process:** Various steps or stages
  This type of organization is used when one event comes before another. The steps may represent cause and effect or they may simply be the order in which something happens. A **flow chart** is a visual representation of this type of organization.
- **Exemplification:** Giving examples
  Abstract concepts frequently need concrete examples in order to be understood. First, the idea is explained, then an example is used to make the idea clearer.
- **Contrast and comparison:** Differences and similarities
  Contrast refers to the differences between things and **comparison** to the similarities. This type of organization is often used when we want to look at two or more products, people, places, or things and then recommend one.
- **Enumeration:** Listing related items
  This is a very common form of organization for all types of writing. While it may be very easy to make a list of all the things we want to say, a better way is to organize by **criteria** and **category**. Also, the order of importance is pertinent here as we must think about the attention of our audience. We will explore this concept further in Chapter 7.
- **Causality:** Explaining cause and effect
  This is different from chronology or process organization because there is a direct causal link drawn between two events. We will look at causality again in Chapter 5.

By organizing the information we want to convey, we lend understanding and credibility to our message.

3) How Will my Audience Read/Listen to and Understand it?

The sender's job is to make the information clear and credible. If our audience can follow the message from one point to another, they are much more likely to believe what we say. Remember that a good opening, when we tell our audience what the message is about, and a good closing, when we ask for action, are two important moments. Our audience will pay more attention at these times so it is important to plan well.

Organizing the Message

 FOCUS ON LANGUAGE

We need three things to make a sentence:

1) A subject
2) A verb
3) A complete thought

A **subject** can be a noun, a pronoun, or even a gerund. It is defined as singular or plural, and may have adjectives or phrases that modify it.

A **verb** can be simple or complex, and in some cases, must change depending on whether the subject is singular or plural.

Forms of the Verb 'Be'

- I (am, was)
- He/she/it (is, was)
- We/you/they (are, were)

Regular and Irregular Verbs

- I/we/you/they (work, come, do, have)
- He/she/it (works, comes, does, has)

The difficulty in matching the subject and verb arises when the sequence, position, or number of the subject is difficult to determine:

Judy works in the public relations office. (Singular subject: Judy)

Judy and Eileen work in the public relations office. (Plural subject: Judy and Eileen)

There are no men in the public relations office. (Plural subject: Men)

The project director of the combined offices comes to work at 8:30 am. (Singular subject: Director)

The children of employees are not allowed in the office canteen. (Plural subject: Children)

Singular and Plural Pronouns

Some indefinite pronouns are singular although we often think of them as plural:

- Anybody (~one, ~thing)
- Everybody (~one, ~thing)
- Somebody (~one, ~thing)
- No one (~body, ~thing)
- Each (one)
- Either
- Neither

'None' is singular in formal writing, but some experts allow it to be used in the plural in informal situations.

Adjectives that make the noun singular are: each, every, any.

Plural pronouns are: few, many.

Everyone wants to be the first at work. (Singular: Everyone)

Any employee knows the rules about children in the canteen. (Singular: Any employee)

A few of the employees were late today because of the rain. (Plural: Few)

Some pronouns can be either singular or plural depending on the context. If the object of the prepositional phrase modifying one of these pronouns is plural, then the verb is plural. Singular or plural pronouns are:

- All
- Any
- Half
- Most
- Part
- Some

Some of the cake is leftover from the company picnic. (Singular: Cake)

Some of the notebooks are ready for collection.
(Plural: Notebooks)

Half of the work is still not finished. (Singular: Work)

All of the assignments you gave me are completed.
(Plural: Assignments)

Countable and Uncountable Nouns

Some nouns are countable and have a plural form as well as a singular form for example, book, books; day, days.

Some nouns, however, are not countable and usually have only one form—the singular. Qualities, processes, topics, and substances are some nouns that are not countable. Examples include intelligence, fear, food, water, news, advice, information, equipment, furniture, money, and research:

Information relating to the mergers is available on our website.
(Singular: Information)

Research into plans for the new building site was done last year.
(Singular: Research)

Collective Nouns

Some collective nouns can be either singular or plural depending on the context. They include team, committee, faculty, family, and staff:

The Welfare Committee handles personal leave requests.
(Singular: Committee)

The team are wonderful players. (Plural: All team members)

The staff eat in the staff canteen (Plural: Staff members)

The front office staff recommends moving the photocopy machine. (Singular: Staff as a whole group)

ACTIVITY: Determining Subject-Verb Agreement

In the following memo are 10 subject-verb agreement mistakes. Underline them and then in the margin, indicate the correct grammar. Check with your group to make sure you have corrected all the errors.

Nanyang Business Associates
Clock Manufacturers to the World

Colin McCarthy, Manager
Gifts from the Forest
Blue Mountain Road
Katoomba 2488 NSW
Australia

Dear Mr. McCarthy,
As the tourist season and warm weather returns to Australia, we are happy to offer our new line of desk clocks to include in your stock. Just to remind you, last year you bought three dozen of our clocks. Because we have a good business relationship, we now offer you the opportunity to select what you want before we offer this line to other businesses.

Each of our clocks are made to a unique design which we are sure your customers will appreciate. Some of the design features is uniquely suited to your tourist area, and most of the workmanship are of the very highest standard.

The most popular of our new desk clocks are made of the best wood. Our team are re-outfitted every year with computer assisted precision tools so that every hand carved detail is beautiful and functional. All of our clocks are tested before they are painted, calibrated and shipped. We provide a guarantee of five years.

Informations regarding these clocks and their guarantees is found on our website. Also, many of our customers logs on to our website which our excellent IT staff have designed for us. Models of the latest clock design, which our master clock designer finished last year, appears on the website as well.

As an expression of our appreciation for your past business, we will pay all of the shipping costs for every clock you order before the end of the year.

With warm wishes,

Project Director

Adapted from Featheringham and Baker. 2001. *Applications in Business Communication*, p.17.

After your group has found and corrected all the errors, assess your own mistakes.

1) Which errors did you not catch?
2) Why?
3) Which ones were easy for you?
4) Which ones were difficult?

As a group, make a list of the most frequent errors you and your team mates have made. This is a chance for you to gain awareness of your own and your team mates' language difficulties.

 FOCUS ON WRITING

When we organize our ideas, we often divide things up into groups of things that are similar. We decide the factor, or **criterion** (look this up in the dictionary for the plural), that we will use to judge the **categories**, or groups of things that are similar to each other in the same way. If we change the criterion, the categories should also change.

ACTIVITY: Determining Criterion and Category

Using the list on the following page (you may photocopy it to make it larger), cut out all the boxes with one animal in each box. Then choose a criterion and divide the animals into categories. Name the categories.

> The criterion is size. The categories will be small, medium, and large.

1) Are these categories adequate for this list of animals?
2) Do you want to add more?
3) What will you name them?
4) How will you decide what animal is in which group?

ACTIVITY: Managing the Zoo

You are the new zoo manager and you must organize these animals in the zoo.

Bat	Horse	Kangaroo
Cat	Goldfish	Snake
Cow	Elephant	Mouse
Lion	Chimpanzee	Dog
Whale	Spider	Canary
Butterfly	Koala	Monkey
Ostrich	Starfish	Bear

1) How many different ways can you think of to display them?
2) How can you organize them for the food supply manager?
3) How would you organize them for the monthly accounts?
4) How can you organize them for the classes of schoolchildren that come to the zoo?
5) Are there any animals that you would not want to have in your zoo? Why?
6) What is the criterion? What are the categories?

Outlines

The following are some key points about writing outlines:

- Process your information before you present it to your reader. The order in which you became aware of information is usually not the best order to present it to your reader.
- When you have lots of information, group it into three to seven categories. The average person's short-term memory can hold only seven chunks, though the chunks can be of any size.
- Work with the reader's expectations, not against them. Introduce ideas in the overview in the order in which you will discuss them.
- When you write an outline, you must make sure that you have two or more points under each category. In other words, if you have an A, you must have a B. Similarly, if you have a 1.1, you must have a 1.2, and so on.

Format for Alphanumeric Outline
Title: Major Idea, Purpose

I First major component
   A. First sub-point
      1. Detail, illustration, evidence
      2. Detail, illustration, evidence
   B. Second sub-point
      1. Detail, illustration, evidence
      2. Detail, illustration, evidence
II Second major component
   A. First sub-point
      1.
      2.

B. Second sub-point
      1.
      2.
III Third major component
   A. First sub-point
      1.
      2.
   B. Second sub-point
      1.
      2.

Format for Decimal Outline
Title: Major Idea, Purpose

1.0 First major component
   1.1 First sub-point
      1.1.1 Detail, illustration, evidence
      1.1.2 Detail, illustration, evidence
   1.2 Second sub-point
      1.2.1 Detail, illustration, evidence
      1.2.2 Detail, illustration, evidence
2.0 Second major component
   2.1 First sub-point
      2.1.1
      2.1.2
   2.2 Second sub-point
      2.2.1
      2.2.2
3.0 Third major component
   3.1 First sub-point
      3.1.1
      3.1.2
   3.2 Second sub-point
      3.2.1
      3.2.2

ACTIVITY: Writing an Outline (Portfolio Assignment)

In conjunction with the Focus on Speaking activity, Designing your Product, following the design of your product, each of you should write an outline of the presentation to the boss.

1) How will you present your product?
2) In what order will you discuss the major points?
3) What kind of thought process will you use to make your points understandable and persuasive to your boss?

FOCUS ON SPEAKING

ACTIVITY: Thinking on your Feet

Practice speaking quickly. You are to write three topics on three small pieces of paper, which your teacher will collect and put in a 'hat.' Use topics that anyone can speak about; for example, best friend, mother, favorite hobby, clothes I like, greatest fear, and so on.

Round 1: In groups, one person chooses a topic from the teacher's hat. Each group has two minutes to brainstorm together. Then one person will give a one-minute presentation on that topic, using the brainstorming ideas gathered by the group.

Round 2: A representative from each group picks a topic from the hat and has one minute to prepare and then one minute to speak on that topic.

Round 3: A representative from each group picks a topic from the hat and has one minute to prepare and then one minute to speak on that topic. (Same as Round 2)

Round 4: A representative from each group picks a topic from the hat and has 15 seconds to prepare and then one minute to speak on that topic.

Round 5: A representative from each group picks a topic from the hat and has no time to prepare but has one minute to speak on that topic.

Round 6: The whole class comes together. Two or three volunteers pick a topic one by one, have 15 seconds to prepare and then speak for 1-2 minutes on that topic.

Round 7: Repeat Round 6.

PERSUASIVE WRITING & SPEAKING

ACTIVITY: Designing your Product

Step 1: Take the market research survey that your group has completed and discuss the results.

1) What kind of shampoo appeals to you?
2) Why?
3) What kind of shampoo might appeal to another market?

Step 2: Design your own shampoo or other product. Include the following information:

Name of product _____

Price per ml _____ Size _____

Shape of container _____

Color of container _____ Color of product _____

Slogan _____

On another piece of paper, draw the container and label for your product. Include pertinent information.

Step 3: Determine the marketing mix. Using the information above, think about what would be a good marketing mix for your product. Try to be as specific as possible.

Target Market _____

Product _____

Price _____

Placement _____

Promotion _____

Step 4: Prepare a presentation to the head of the marketing division explaining your product and why you think it would be a good one for the company. Two or three group members should do the presentation at the next lesson.

Adapted from Arden and Dowling. 1993. *Business Concepts for English Practice*, p.45.

Step 5: See the activity, Writing an Outline (Portfolio Assignment), in the Focus on Writing section.

FOCUS ON REFLECTION

In the Focus on Communication section of this chapter, we looked at a number of thought processes or different ways to organize our message.

1) Which of these methods have you used?
2) Which ones might you consider for the portfolio assignment?
3) Which one did you use when you wrote your introduction letter?
4) Is there another way of organizing this information?

In Focus on Language, we looked at subject-verb agreement.

1) Which situation gives you the most trouble?
2) Why?
3) What can you do to make sure you do not make the same kind of mistakes in the future?

In the Focus on Writing segment, we did some activities that helped us look further into organizing our work.

1) Are you clearer now about criterion and category?
2) How can these concepts help you to make sense of your ideas?
3) How can outlining your work first make it easier to write?

In Focus on Speaking, we had a chance to practice our skills.

1) Do you feel more confident now if you are asked to say something in public?
2) Have you obtained any new ideas about how to prepare quickly to make sense of your thoughts?
3) When you discussed ideas with your team mates about your product, did you try to get everyone's ideas?
4) Why should you?

chapter 4

Structure and Transitions

 FOCUS ON COMMUNICATION

Before we start on any journey, we should know where it will end. We do not go to the train station and simply board any train that comes along. Instead, we plan our destination and any transfers along the way. We also make sure we know at which platform the train we want to take stops. Then, as we travel on the train, we take note of the stations that we pass through, periodically checking to make sure where we are in relation to our final destination. If we have to transfer to another train, we need to know where to get off and which train to get on next. Before we reach our destination, we need to collect our things and prepare to get off. If we neglect to plan our journey, we are likely to be delayed or even end up at the wrong destination.

Writing a message can be compared with a train journey. We need to plan where to start, where to make transitions, and when to stop. We need to know what our goal is so we can successfully reach it in the best way possible. We do not want to waste our time and our message receiver's time by failing to plan ahead.

In persuasive messages, we usually let our reader know at the beginning what our message is, and then we proceed to build our argument. We make claims and support them with examples and illustrations. We may also include information about the opposite point of view to counter any arguments from another perspective.

In this chapter, we will look at the ways we show transition from one topic to another and how we mark the 'stations' along the way.

FOCUS ON LANGUAGE

Now that we have reviewed verbs and verb tenses and have also identified subjects and verbs and their possible disagreements, we can look at another area of consistency. This is maintaining consistent time in our verb tenses.

If we are describing current events or something that affects the present time, we can say we have a present time frame. If we are describing things that happened in the past, we have a past time frame. Sometimes we want to describe events in the past that caused the present situation or that definitely happened before the current event. In that case, we may have both a present and a past time frame even within one sentence. But we must be careful not to change our verb tense with no reason. It may make our work unnecessarily hard to read and may be confusing to the receiver. This problem may lead to misunderstanding and loss of credibility, both of which we want to avoid.

The basic way we decide the time frame we will write our message in is by looking at the first verb in the text. If it is in the present time frame, then we should be consistently in the present; if it is in the past time frame, then our verbs should be in the past tense:

EXAMPLE 1: Present time frame
Special activity groups have become (present perfect) very popular among young singles. These groups help (simple present) their members meet other singles and enjoy activities.

EXAMPLE 2: Past time frame
Before Johan graduated (simple past) from university, he had worked (past perfect) at the campus newspaper office for two years. Because he had (simple past) experience, he looked (simple past) for a job in publishing.

Time Frame Shifts

Sometimes we use both time frames within a text to indicate a shift from past to present or present to past. We can use a shift from the present to the past to contrast the present situation with the past, or to explain the present by descriptions or examples that occurred in the past.

Often the present tense verbs—the simple present and the present perfect—are used to frame topics. The information about what we think, feel, or believe is true is often in a present time frame, whereas descriptions of events are in the past time frame:

EXAMPLE 1: Present to past time frame shift
The general office staff has instituted (present perfect) some simple rules for the regular supply of stationary items. In the past, staff members took (simple past) what they wanted (simple past) from the open shelves. This led (simple past) to abuses of the honor system.

This example contrasts the present situation (rules) with the past situation (honor system):

EXAMPLE 2: Past to present time frame shift
Last year, our company witnessed (simple past) a decrease in the petty pilfering of office supplies. We also noticed (simple past) a decline in the wastage of paper. We need (simple present) to continue these cost-saving trends in order to weather the current economic downturn.

Notice the shift from a past tense describing events in the past year, to a present tense statement.

ACTIVITY: Maintaining Consistency in Tense Usage

1) In the following text are four tense mistakes. Underline them and then in the margin, indicate the correct tense. Check with your group to make sure you have corrected all the errors.

> About Impress Gum
>
> Impress Gum is located in Santa Barbara, California. Impress Gum developed and marketed functional chewing gums that enhance health and well-being. The company is dedicated to providing a high quality functional chewing gum that tasted great. Impress Gum freshens breath, whitens teeth and helps prevent tooth decay. The Heath Sciences Authority, Singapore has granted a product license for Impress Gum to be imported and sold. For more information on Impress Gum, please reference the company's website at www.impressgum.com.

> About Kingston Medical Supplies
>
> Kingston Medical Supplies (Pte) Ltd was located in Singapore. The company is in the business of importing and distributing Medical Equipment, Instruments and Medical Sundries, and Home Healthcare Products.

2) The following text has nine grammatical mistakes. Underline them and then in the margin, indicate the correct form. Check with your group to make sure you have corrected **all** the errors.

> A large city like Singapore offers visitors many kinds of exciting activities. If someone wanted to attend sporting events, a large city usually have professional soccer teams. If visitors did not care for sports, perhaps museums filled the bill. A large city usually has art museums as well as historical and cultural museums. For the visitor who liked shopping, the large city provided a range of stores from small specialty shops to large department stores. Since Singapore is near the water, it offered river boat cruises, a harbor cruise, beaches, aquariums and other waterfront activities. Theaters and nightclubs also gave visitors a chance to experience evening entertainment they did not have at home. A large city gives an out-of-town visitor a wide range of activities for excitement and fun.

Adapted from Wingersky, Boerner, and Holguin-Balogh. 2003. *Writing Paragraphs and Essays*, p.81.

After your group has found and corrected all the errors in the two extracts, assess your own mistakes.

1) Which errors did you not catch?
2) Why?
3) Which ones were easy for you?
4) Which ones were difficult?

As a group, make a list of the most frequent errors you and your team mates have made. This is a chance for you to gain awareness of your own and your team mates' language difficulties.

FOCUS ON WRITING

Transition markers are used to signal changes from one topic to another and to move the text along. In English, we use many more transition markers than in some Asian languages such as Chinese.

- To show **chronology**, use: in, on, at (plus specific times), then, at that point, after that, afterwards, before, meanwhile, during, when, by the time, as.
- To show **sequence**, use: first, second, third, next, finally, then, one reason (example), another reason (example), most important, in conclusion.
- To signal **examples**, use: for example, for instance.
- To show **contrast** or **comparison**, use: similarly, likewise, however, in the same way, on the other hand, in contrast, in comparison.
- To show **addition**, use: also, furthermore, another (example, point, step…), in addition, next.
- To show **causality**, use: therefore, consequently, as a result, because, because of, for this reason, hence, since.

ACTIVITY: Peer Editing – Adding Transition Markers

Exchange outlines with a team mate.

1) Where would you add transition markers?
2) Why?
3) Do you need transition markers in every sentence?

ACTIVITY: Self-Editing

Look at your first portfolio assignment.

1) Can you find any transition markers?
2) Where?
3) Which ones did you use?
4) What do they signal?
5) Can you add more for smoother reading?

Discuss the following with your team mates:

1) Which transition markers are easiest to use?
2) Why?

3) Which ones are the most difficult?
4) Why?

Headings, Bullet Points, and Numbers

Business writing differs from essay writing in the way we organize our message. Business writing is characterized by headings used as transition markers, bullet points, and lists using numbers.

Headings

Headings are used to break up long texts. They should be descriptive and make a statement:

> Recommendation (Does not make a statement)
>
> Recommendation to make Tan Hui Ling our representative (Descriptive)

Headings should also maintain parallelism:

> Choosing a qualified candidate for representative
>
> Electing our representative democratically
>
> Maintaining continuity key to success

Bullet points and numbers

Items can be listed using bullet points or numbers, making reading and understanding the message faster and easier:

> When writing an email, keep these pointers in mind.
> - Use formal English spelling, not spelling used in SMS
> - Avoid SHOUTING
> - Proofread all messages before they are sent
> - Wait before you send an angry message
>
> For the next meeting of the board, the administrative assistant needs to do the following:
> 1) Reserve the conference room
> 2) Send invitations
> 3) Arrange for coffee and tea service
> 4) Make name badges for all participants

ACTIVITY: Writing a Feedback Memo (Portfolio Assignment)

Write a memo to your classmate giving feedback on his/her speaking presentation. (See activity, Doing a Team Presentation of New Product, in the Focus on Speaking section of this chapter.) In the memo, evaluate his/her speech and give recommendations for improvement. Remember to think about criteria and categories for evaluation.

You also need to think about how you will organize the message. Do not forget to think about who your audience is and what he/she will feel about your message on receiving it.

Portfolios

Portfolios are collections of your work. They are used by artists or other professionals to show what they have done. Below are some answers to questions you may have.

What goes in my portfolio?

As you write your assignments every week, you submit them to your teacher for feedback. He/she corrects your errors and returns each assignment to you. Then you should rewrite them and place them in the portfolio sleeve for that assignment. All versions, original and corrected ones, should be filed in the same sleeve. Other material can also be put into your portfolio. If you are proud of a grammar exercise, practice essay, or some other work pertaining to the class, you may include it. This should be listed under 'Other Work.'

What should I use as a portfolio?

A summary sheet of your portfolio (see next page) should be reproduced and then updated every time you complete a portfolio assignment. File it into the first sleeve of your portfolio. You will need a book or folder, preferably a 20-pocket clear book to put all your assignments in.

Why do I need a portfolio?

Your portfolio is a record of your work for the semester. On a personal basis, it shows your progress through the semester. By looking at your first and last portfolio entries, you should be able to see improvements. For assessment purposes, your teacher can see what you have accomplished and whether you have mastered the skills presented.

My Portfolio Assignments

Name:

Tutorial number:

Assignment number	Title or description	Date submitted	Date revised

 **FOCUS ON SPEAKING**

ACTIVITY: Doing a Team Presentation of New Product

Each team should designate two or three members to give a short presentation of your new product. Below is a checklist of important elements of a good presentation. You can use ideas from this list to complete your writing assignment. (See the Focus on Writing activity, Writing a Feedback Memo.)

Speaking Evaluation

The Speech Evaluation Checklist has four components:

- Language control
- Vocal variety
- Body language
- Organization

Language control refers to the ability to be understood by the listeners. It includes articulation and diction, as well as the number of distracters that interrupt the flow of speech. Rhythm and stress are important features of English that contribute to understanding. Poor pronunciation includes dropping the ends of words so the listener does not know whether the speaker is aware of the correct grammar or just has poor pronunciation. Grammatical errors that interfere with the credibility of the speaker are also part of this component.

Vocal variety refers to the emphasis given by pacing, volume, and change of pitch. A speaker's enthusiasm comes through vocal variety. If a speaker speaks too quickly or too slowly, we fall asleep or become bored.

Body language encompasses gestures, eye contact, facial expression, animation, poise, and posture. Delivery includes the concept of contact with the audience. Appropriate appearance includes dressing, hairstyle, grooming, and accessories. If we are interesting to watch, our message gets through. Appearance that is distracting or inappropriate may cause credibility problems.

Organization refers to how well our ideas are organized. The introduction, transition markers, conclusion, and reasoning behind the ideas are all part of making the presentation comprehensible. In speaking, listeners have no chance to 'go back' and listen again; they must be kept informed at all times when the speaker is in the presentation.

PERSUASIVE WRITING & SPEAKING

The Speaking Evaluation Checklist

	Language Control	Vocal Variety	Body Language	Organization
5-6	Excellent articulation, correct pronunciation, appropriate stress, and rhythm. No distracters that interrupt the flow of speech. No errors that affect credibility.	Confidence and enthusiasm displayed. Appropriate volume, excellent pacing, pitch, range, and variety.	Poised and confident posture. Excellent eye contact. Purposeful gestures that complement and enhance meaning. Animated facial expressions. Highly appropriate appearance.	Clear signals of organization, i.e., clear introduction, advanced organizers, transition markers, conclusion.
3-4	Acceptable pronunciation, but articulation may not be as clear, often because speech is too fast. There are occasional distracters.	Some confidence and enthusiasm is displayed. Some variety in rhythm, pacing, pitch, and range is noticeable.	Posture may be slightly awkward. Facial expressions may lack some animation, but gestures and appearance are appropriate. Some eye contact with audience is made.	A number of signals of organization, but could improve with more.
1-2	Poor pronunciation, which creates misunderstanding and damages credibility. Very frequent deletion of word endings. Staccato rhythm and frequent distracters.	Monotonous, as there is no variety, thus putting listeners to sleep.	No gestures, no eye contact. Highly distracting mannerisms. Inappropriate or highly distracting dress or grooming.	Key elements of organization are omitted such that ideas may be incomprehensible to the audience.

FOCUS ON REFLECTION

In this chapter, we looked at one very valuable learning strategy: reflection on our classmates' work and on our own work. By reviewing our work critically, we can make it better. This is a skill that needs to be practiced every time we speak or write. By involving our classmates, we can use their perspective as well as our own in order to get a variety of opinions. This can lead to a more accurate assessment of our work.

In Focus on Language, we explored the concept of consistency in verb tenses.

1) Is this a new concept for you?
2) Are you confident you can control your time frames?
3) If not, what can you do to correct this?

In Focus on Writing for the previous chapter, we started on ways to organize our writing. In this chapter, we continued with the concept of transition markers, headings, bullet points, and numbers as ways to make our writing easier to understand.

1) Do you feel you can control your transition markers?
2) Are you able to vary them as the type of writing changes?
3) Can you identify good headings?
4) Do you know when to use bullet points and numbers?

In Focus on Speaking, we were introduced to the Speaking Evaluation Checklist and asked to use the ideas to evaluate our peers.

1) Are there any of the speech evaluation points you do not understand?
2) Which one(s)?
3) Are you able to recognize when a speaker has given a good presentation?
4) Which of these categories do you think is the most important?

chapter 5

Reasoning

 FOCUS ON COMMUNICATION

When we create an argument, we want to explain the reasons for our view. We may need to explain process or cause and effect in order to strengthen our position.

The first thing that needs to be established with our receiver is common ground. If we analyze our audience and can determine how they feel about the topic, we can then construct an argument that begins with something the sender and receiver share. For example, buyers and sellers want to make a deal and everyone in a company wants the company to do well. By starting from a goal that both parties want to achieve, or a common belief or assumption about the topic, the sender can then begin the argument.

When making an argument, the writer or speaker starts with a position or claim. This claim needs to be clearly stated, but should not contain any more than can be supported by the evidence. We need to be careful of absolutes, such as 'always' and 'never,' and claims of evaluation, such as the best, the highest, or the greatest. We should only claim what we can support.

We must also avoid fallacies. A **fallacy** is an idea based on incorrect information or reasoning. A few common fallacies are listed below with examples:

- **Ad hominem** is a fallacy that attacks the person who puts forth the idea rather than the idea itself:

    It was the VP of Marketing who brought that idea to our attention. It is obviously a stupid one because we all know that the VP knows nothing about finance.

- **Ad populum** refers to the popularity of an idea. If everyone believes this idea is right, then it cannot be wrong:

    Coca-Cola is the best cola in the world because everybody drinks it.

- **Begging the question** is a circular argument that states that something is true because it is true:

    Marissa is sure to get the position as office manager because she is so efficient. We know she is efficient because she is sure to get the position.

- **Hasty generalization** is a fallacy that depends on too few examples or isolated ones. Statistics must be based on a large enough sample size to be useful and this is one way in which we must be cautious when stating generalizations:

    Young college graduates these days do not write or speak well. Four of them applied for jobs here last week and none of them had a properly written CV.

- A **post hoc** fallacy, sometimes called a **false cause** fallacy, is one where a causal link between two events is assumed. Inexperienced researchers often draw conclusions based on statistical correlation without thoroughly investigating the cause and effect:

    All of the top executives belong to the Pacific Asian Club. If you want to be successful and become a top executive in the company, you need to join this club.

- **Slippery slope** is a fallacy that asserts that taking the first step automatically leads to a second (or third) undesirable step:

    Oil companies have been caught too many times using faulty tankers to transport oil. We need to stop the use of oil tankers because oil spills harm the environment. Once an oil spill has occurred, beaches become unusable, wildlife dies, fishing is disrupted, and the local economy suffers. Once the local economy suffers…

When making claims and citing support, we must be sure our logic is correct and that our examples are adequate and pertinent. Our credibility rests on the trustworthiness of our arguments.

 FOCUS ON LANGUAGE

Causality is the relationship of cause and effect. We can imply causality by the relationship of two events in a sentence, one after the other. However, to be clear and precise, we need to use the vocabulary and structures of causality.

We can organize information about the causes, reasons, sources, motives, or objectives of something either before or after the effect:

> Because 10cm of rain fell last night, the central expressway was flooded this morning. (Cause, then effect)

> The central expressway was flooded this morning as a result of the heavy rain last night. (Effect, then cause)

The two ideas of cause and effect, while they can be placed in either position in the sentence, use different grammatical structures:

> The electricity to Block A will be cut off next Monday morning for repairs to the system; therefore all employees who work in Block A will report to Block B instead. (Cause, then effect)

> Because there will be no electricity next Monday morning in Block A, all employees in that block should report to Block B. (Cause, then effect)

> All Block A employees will report to Block B on Monday morning because Block A will have no electricity. (Effect, then cause)

Note that 'because,' 'since,' and 'as,' when used in a clause at the beginning of a sentence, have a comma after the clause. If they are used in a clause at the end of a sentence, there is no comma. See the examples above. Whenever we start a sentence with 'because,' we must be sure to check that we have a complete thought. For this, we will generally need a cause and an effect, not just a cause.

Articles

Because many Asian languages do not have articles, the simple 'a,' 'an,' and 'the' can cause lots of confusion. To maintain clarity and completeness, article use needs to be mastered.

Basic rules for articles

- 'A' and 'an' are indefinite articles; 'the' is definite.
- 'An' is used when the following word begins with a vowel sound.

    An application

    An educated worker

    An honest word

    A university

Indefinite articles are general determiners indicating that the noun is a representative of a class or group. We use them when we refer to something for the first time or when we use individuals to generalize about the class of things to which it belongs:

   The secretary asked me to buy a notebook. (Unspecified)

On the other hand, the **definite article** 'the' is used to identify a specific item that has already been mentioned or alluded to in the text. It can also be used to refer to one thing only, specific places and organizations, generalizations, superlatives, general determiners, and numbers:

   The notebook (already mentioned) I bought from the campus bookstore (specific place) cost $3.00. It was the best (superlative) one available.

Singular nouns can take 'a' or 'an,' but plural nouns cannot. Singular and plural nouns can take 'the.' Uncountable nouns can only take 'the,' never 'a' or 'an.'

The **'zero' article** (no article) is used with uncountable nouns and most proper nouns when we introduce something the first time or are speaking generally. We do not use an article before meals, days of the week, or institutions:

The patience (uncountable) to operate the machine (specific) is important.

Some argue that democracy (general) is an essential part (first mention) of good government (general).

The hotel (specific) does not usually serve breakfast (meal) on Sunday (day of the week).

ACTIVITY: Finding and Correcting the Errors

In the following passage, choose 'a,' 'an,' 'the,' or leave blank. Check your work with your team mates when you have finished.

Sportco Ltd: _____ Career Choice

J.M. Sun is _____ senior product marketing manager for _____ highly successful line of _____ athletic wear known _____ worldwide by its trademarked logo. He has just received _____ phone call from _____ division's vice president, who is his boss. After _____ usual pleasantries and _____ discussion of some 'hot' issues, _____ vice president invites him to _____ lunch _____ next day.

Earlier _____ fax had been passed to Mr. Sun concerning _____ new vacancy in _____ key overseas regional office. This position is for _____ regional marketing manager, and it is _____ important step to moving upward within _____ Sportco Ltd's marketing division.

Mr. Sun has _____ difficult decision to make. _____ new job overseas would mean _____ 20 percent pay increase, plus _____ very generous overseas living allowance. However, _____ regional marketing manager position requires _____ three-year commitment.

PERSUASIVE WRITING & SPEAKING

> Mr. Sun has _____ number of concerns. First, he is afraid of being so far away from _____ corporate headquarters and does not want to lose his connection with _____ successful athletic product line. Second, he is worried about _____ impact on his family – his wife, 9-year-old son, and 12-year-old daughter. Finally, he is not sure what _____ next career step would be after _____ overseas assignment. Yet after _____ 16 years with _____ Sportco Ltd and four years in his current position, he is looking for _____ new challenges.

Adapted from Arden and Dowling. 1993. *Business Concepts for English Practice*, p.22.

After your group has found and corrected all the errors, assess your own mistakes.

1) Which errors did you not catch?
2) Why?
3) Which ones were easy for you?
4) Which ones were difficult?

As a group, make a list of the most frequent errors you and your team mates have made.

 FOCUS ON WRITING

Writing Evaluation

This Writing Evaluation Checklist has three components:
- Language control
- Organization and coherence
- Content

Language control refers to the grammar and tone of the writing. Spelling, punctuation, correct grammar, and appropriate word choices contribute to good language control.

Organization and **coherence** are necessary for the reader to understand the message. There is a clear beginning, middle, and end that are linked together with proper transition markers. Sentences are neither too long nor too short, and they flow from one to the other so as to be easily understood.

Content includes the articulation of the main idea with sufficient supporting evidence. A piece of writing with good content is written for a particular audience and the issues are presented in such a way as to inform, persuade, argue, and so on.

For writing to be effective, all elements need to be controlled and mastered. Use the following chart to assess your own and your partner's writing.

The Writing Evaluation Checklist

Level	Language Control	Organization and Coherence	Content
5-6	Excellent grammar and syntax. No noticeable spelling, punctuation, or grammatical errors. Precise, varied, and appropriate vocabulary.	Excellent organization and control of transitions. Reader is always aware of direction of the argument. No confusion between claim and support.	Issues are clearly and fully dealt with. Claims are supported by clear and appropriate statements. Arguments are substantial and not trivial.
3-4	Good language control, but some noticeable errors that can interfere with comprehension. Good but limited vocabulary.	Good organization, but may be lacking in overall coherence. Some parts may be connected, but other places may show muddy transitions or lack of control of organization.	Claims and support are evident, but there may be a lack of focus or development. There may be repetition or inconsistency.
1-2	Language control is noticeably lacking. Frequent grammatical or spelling errors interfere with message, causing confusion and misunderstanding. Limited vocabulary that lacks precision.	Lack of organization and control of transitions. Reader may find it difficult to follow the topic and supporting points.	The topic is dealt with, but ideas are not presented clearly or supported with evidence. There may be extraneous or erroneous material.

ACTIVITY: Peer Reviewing

Exchange your portfolio assignment from the previous class with your partner. Using the Writing Evaluation Checklist, review your partner's memo.

1) Is the memo written with correct grammar? (Review verb tenses, subject-verb agreement, articles, etc.)
2) Does the memo use precise and varied vocabulary?
3) Point out some good language use to your partner.
4) How is the memo organized?
5) Are transition markers used?
6) Where?
7) Are there enough to follow the memo throughout?
8) Did the writer deal with all the issues?
9) Did the writer include both praise for a good speech and suggestions for improvement?
10) Give examples.

ACTIVITY: Writing about Cause and Effect (Portfolio Assignment)

Write an email to your teacher explaining why you missed your last two classes. Be sure to:

1) Analyze your audience
2) Organize your email
3) Review it carefully for completeness and clarity

 FOCUS ON SPEAKING

Team Work

The modern business world increasingly uses small groups working in teams on projects, so being able to successfully work with others is a crucial business skill. Small groups often meet, and so being able to hold successful meetings is also crucial to the ultimate goal of completing projects on time.

When forming a team, remember that diversity gives a variety of views. Although it may be difficult at first to accommodate differing viewpoints, in the end, the product is better.

Effective leadership is important for smooth working relationships and final project success. Good leaders strive to be neutral and objective, help the group progress, delegate responsibility, and encourage team members. An effective way of working is for someone to initially take the role of leader, and then pass it along to another group member so that responsibilities and experiences are shared.

Teams do not always function smoothly. They are characterized by 'life cycles' that change from one stage to another as members get to know one another, disagree, negotiate, and solve problems. The key to working successfully as a team includes **listening effectively**, dealing with **social loafing**, **groupthink**, and overcoming socio-cultural differences, which are brought about by differences in age, ethnicity, experience, and gender; for example, women in general are less likely to interrupt or take the floor, and prefer collaboration. On the other hand, men tend to interrupt more often, take the floor and hold it longer, are more verbally aggressive, and prefer to work independently.

Meetings are held in different places: in the classroom, in a café, in someone's room, via telephone or the Internet. The purpose varies from informational to problem-solving. It is best to make sure before the group meets that everyone knows the purpose, the agenda, who is responsible for facilitating the meeting, who is to take notes, and who will assign follow-up actions. By encouraging healthy debate, avoiding dominance by one person, listening attentively, and making decisions, teams can successfully complete their work.

ACTIVITY: Discussing Group Work

During your last group meeting:

1) Did you have a leader/facilitator?
2) Did you have an agenda?
3) Did you have someone to take notes?
4) Did you end with an action plan?
5) Give an example of effective listening from your last group meeting.
6) Did you have any social loafers?
7) Has your group ever engaged in groupthink? When?
8) What was the outcome?
9) Identify a specific example of gender differences in your group.
10) How did you manage your last group conflict?

ACTIVITY: Creating a Market Research Survey

Now that you have devised a new shampoo (or some other product), you need to design and conduct a market research survey to find out what your consumers' preferences are. As a group, think of the questions you need to ask your customers about your product. Make a list, and then devise a survey form.

After you have made a form, each of you should survey at least 10 people, preferably in the target group. Bring your results to the next class.

FOCUS ON REFLECTION

In this chapter, we looked at cause and effect and the fallacies that can creep into our reasoning.

1) What are the causes of poor language?
2) What are the effects?
3) What action can you take to attack and/or reverse the causes?

In Focus on Language, we briefly covered the use of articles.

1) On a scale of 1 to 10 (with 1 being the easiest), rate how difficult article use is for you.
2) How about as a group?
3) How can you be better at identifying when you need an article?

In Focus on Writing, we were introduced to the Writing Evaluation Checklist.

1) Is this a useful tool for you?
2) Why or why not?
3) What does reviewing your classmates' written work do for you?

In Focus on Speaking, we discussed working in groups and then we worked in a group on an activity.

1) How important is group or team work in your career as a student?
2) As a worker?
3) What do you find easy about working in a team?
4) What do you find difficult?

chapter 6

Supporting the Argument

 FOCUS ON COMMUNICATION

When we make a claim, we need to provide support in the form of evidence. The amount of evidence and how strong it needs to be, varies with the situation. In the case of a murder trial, the evidence needs to be much stronger to convince the judge and jury than in a case of an employee who is late going in to work. In all cases, however, support must be **relevant** to the situation, used in a **convincing** way, and **specific** enough to sway the audience.

The relevance of evidence to the argument must be made clear to the audience. Just because we have consulted other sources or carried out research does not mean that everything we know about a subject is essential to the argument. Removing unnecessary evidence can make our arguments stronger by making them clearer.

Convincing evidence comes from recognized experts and proper research. As well as being relevant and convincing, the evidence needs to be specific enough to illustrate the thesis. Conclusions drawn from evidence should only be as strong as the evidence allows. The difference between something found on the Internet and a study published in a respected academic journal illustrates this point. What is the source? How reliable is it? Is it something that has been reported by one person, or something researched under laboratory conditions?

Seldom can we absolutely prove anything, so the use of absolute terms is something we should avoid. It is advisable to use more tentative vocabulary such as may, might, could, would, possibly, perhaps, probably, although, and while. We are more likely to sway our audience by being honest about our claims and where the support comes from.

PERSUASIVE WRITING & SPEAKING

 FOCUS ON LANGUAGE

As well as indicating an action, a state of being or time, verbs also convey meaning relating to ability, certainty, obligation, and advice. This is done by using modal auxiliary verbs such as can, could, will, would, must, should, may, and might.

Will and Would

We will explore these two modals in this chapter.

'Will' is used in the following situations:

1) To indicate the future

   I will help you write the report next week.

2) To indicate a request

   Will you return my book to the library for me?

3) To indicate the future in the conditional situation in which the speaker sees the consequence as a real possibility

   If the shipment comes in today, we will start our project tomorrow.

'Would' is used in the following situations:

1) To indicate a request that is more polite than 'will'

   Would you please deposit your folders in the general office?

2) To indicate the past tense of 'will' in the conditional situation in which the speaker sees the consequence as a remote possibility or even an impossibility

   If the shipment came in today, we would start the project tomorrow. (Remote possibility)

If the shipment had come in yesterday, we would have started the project today. (An impossibility as the shipment did not come in yesterday)

3) To express likes and preferences

I would like to take a short vacation in the next three weeks.

Stella would prefer not to see any new clients this week.

Below is a summary of the three conditions described above and the verb tenses and forms used in each situation.

Condition	'If' clause verb tense	Main clause verb tense
Possibility	Present simple	Future 'will'
Remote possibility	Past simple	Conditional 'would'
Impossibility	Past perfect	Past conditional 'would have'
Universal conditions*	Present simple	Present simple

*This takes the present tense.

If a company has a sound management team, dealing with emergencies is simple.

ACTIVITY: Finding and Correcting the Errors – 'Will' and 'Would'

There are seven uses of 'will' and 'would' that are incorrect or could have been used better. Watch out for other errors as well. Underline them and then in the margin, indicate the correct grammar. Check with your group to make sure you have corrected all the errors.

> Kris Kliszewicz, a successful businessman in England, has been raising money and interest around the world for a pet project. Kliszewicz wants to build a theme park which would allow people to immerse themselves for a day in the life and times of Shakespeare. He is planning to call the new park, 'Shakespeare's World.'
>
> "If visitors had lived in Shakespeare's day, what would they have seen? What daily sounds will they have heard? What kind of food will they have

61

> eaten? I want to give modern-day Shakespeare lovers the chance to experience daily life as it would have been lived," said Kliszewicz.
>
> Kliszewicz has decided on the perfect location for the first of these parks – on the outskirts of Shakespeare's hometown, Stratford-upon-Avon. At Shakespeare's World, troupes of roaming actors will perform scenes from Shakespeare's plays. According to Kliszewicz, visitors would see the sights and hear the sounds that Shakespeare saw and heard. There would be cobblestone streets complete with bakeries and butcheries, fields full of animals and farming peasants, and trades people who will demonstrate Tudor crafts.
>
> Some Shakespeare scholars are not convinced that a Shakespeare theme park would be a good idea. But Kliszewicz believe that people might enjoy learning more about Shakespeare without the purely academic treatment that is given in classrooms. The idea of Shakespeare's World is also getting attention in China, Russia, and America, which Kliszewicz would plan to make future sites for Shakespeare's World.

Adapted from Wilson and Glazier. 2004. *The Least You Should Know About English*, pp.93–94.

After your group has found and corrected all the errors, assess your own mistakes.

1) Which errors did you not catch?
2) Why?
3) Which ones were easy for you?
4) Which ones were difficult?

As a group, make a list of the most frequent errors you and your team mates have made. This is a chance for you to gain awareness of your own and your team mates' language difficulties.

Probability

In presenting our support, we should try to use certainty and impossibility only when the situation is an absolute. For other situations when we want to present our support as stronger or not as strong, we can use other terms.

- For **certainty**, use: sure, certain, positive, bound to.
- For **probability** (80–90%), use: very likely, probable, should.
- For **possibility** (30–70%), use: may, might.
- For **improbability**, use: unlikely, improbable.
- For **impossibility**, use: sure, certain positive, can + not.

> According to recent trends, it is probable that the company will post a loss again this year. (Probability)

> We may experience minor interruptions to the upward trends, but we are on the road to recovery. (Possibility)

> We are positive that the shipment will not go out today. (Impossibility)

Contrast and Comparison

Using transition markers and connectors are ways to make meaning clearer. In using contrast and comparison for illustration and support of claims, we need to use the appropriate terms.

- For **contrast**, use: however, in contrast, on the other hand, though, not as…(adjective)…as, (comparative adjective)…than.
- For **contrast with reservations**, use: even so, however, nevertheless, nonetheless, despite, in spite of, on the other hand.
- For **comparison**, use: likewise, similarly, in the same way, as well, also, like, as…as.

> The US has led the world in technological innovations that change the way the business world works. However, the emerging economies of China and India are set to challenge this dominance. (Contrast between past and future)

> Europeans are proud of their individual cultural heritages and are reluctant to part with familiar things like money. Nonetheless, the euro has become a useful and important common currency in Europe. (Contrast with reservation, the first statement is true, but so is the second)

> Political alliances, such as the EU, have brought countries closer together than before. (Contrast using the comparative adjective) Likewise, these alliances have brought closer economic ties. (Comparison of two ways)

FOCUS ON WRITING

Contrast and Comparison

There are various ways to organize contrast and comparison in text.

Method 1

One way is to discuss the various points of contrast or comparison in alternating paragraphs or section. The criterion is introduced, and then a full description is given first for one item. This is followed by a new paragraph or section for the second item:

I   Introduction to topic, points of similarity/difference
II Body
    A. First point of similarity/difference
       i. Item 1
      ii. Item 2
    B. Second point of similarity
       i. Item 1
      ii. Item 2
    C. Third point
    Etc.
III Conclusion, summary of main points

Method 2

Another way of organization is to include the items within the same paragraph using alternate sentences, or even within the same sentence. This method can be used when comparison or contrast is needed on many smaller points:

I   Introduction to topic, points of similarity/difference
II Body
    A. First point of similarity/difference
       i. Sub-point 1
          1. Item 1
          2. Item 2
      ii. Sub-point 2
          1. Item 1
          2. Item 2

    B. Second point of similarity
        i. Sub-point 1
            1. Item 1
            2. Item 2
        ii. Sub-point 2
            1. Item 1
            2. Item 2
    Etc.
III Conclusion, summary of main points

Method 3

If the items under consideration have some similarities and some contrasts and we want to look at both, then the organization can look like this:

I   Introduction to topic, points of similarity/difference
II Body
    A. Basis of similarity
        i. Point of similarity 1
            1. Item 1
            2. Item 2
        ii. Point of similarity 2
            1. Item 1
            2. Item 2
    B. Basis of contrast
        i. Point of contrast 1
            1. Item 1
            2. Item 2
        ii. Point of contrast 2
            1. Item 1
            2. Item 2
    Etc.
III Conclusion, summary of main points

    This is a particularly good method when making a recommendation. For example, if we want to recommend Product B over Product A, we can show how they are similar in the first part. Then, in subsequent sections, we can show how they are different, emphasizing the particular aspects of Product B that make it better than product A. The persuasiveness of a recommendation depends in part on the organization of the argument.

Persuasive patterns

Some persuasive patterns are outlined below.

Claim pattern

1. Claim 1 (with support)
2. Claim 2 (with support)
3. Claim 3 (with support)

Causal pattern

1. Cause
2. Effect
3. Solution or action

Problem solution pattern

1. Problem
2. Solution
3. Benefits or action

Comparative advantages

1. Plan X is ineffective or average
2. Plan Y is better

Adapted from Hamilton and Parker. 2001. *Communicating for Results.* p.46.

ACTIVITY: Peer Reviewing

Exchange emails with your partner and answer the following questions:

1) Is the memo written with correct grammar? (Review verb tenses, subject-verb agreement, articles, etc.)
2) Does the memo use precise and varied vocabulary?
3) Point out some good language use to your partner.

4) How is the memo organized?
5) Is there a statement of common ground? Where?
6) Are transition markers used? Where?
7) If you were the recipient of this email, would you be convinced?
8) What did the writer say to convince you?
9) Was it based on logos, pathos, or ethos?
10) How effective was the writer in analyzing the audience?

ACTIVITY: Writing a Report (Portfolio Assignment)

Based on the surveys that your team has collected on your product, write a recommendation memo to your project director. (Complete the activity for Focus on Speaking before you write the memo. You may include the entire group's information or only your own.)

If you recommend changes to your product, why? Be sure to keep in mind organizational patterns that enhance the persuasive value of the memo.

 FOCUS ON SPEAKING

By keeping in mind the factors that make teams work well, we can practice effective team work every time we meet. Soon, holding good meetings will become second nature.

ACTIVITY: Analyzing your Market Research Survey

In your group, pool your questionnaires and find out potential customers' reaction to your product.

1) Did your target audience like it?
2) Why or why not?
3) Do you want to change anything about your product?
4) What?
5) How?

The answers to your market survey and possible recommendations will be used in writing your recommendation report (see Focus on Writing.)

ACTIVITY: Advertising your Product

Now that you have designed and redesigned your product, it is time to market it.

1) Who is your target market?
2) Why should they buy it?
3) How can you convince them? Logos? Pathos? Ethos?

Design a short (30 seconds to 1 minute long) radio or TV advertisement for your product. Discuss these questions first:

1) Do you have a favorite TV or radio advertisement?
2) What do you like about it?
3) How is it organized? How does it start?
4) When is the product introduced?
5) Is there a 'punch line'?

Now you are ready to create an advertisement. Choose two or three representatives from your team to read or act out the advertisement.

FOCUS ON REFLECTION

In this chapter, we continued to look at the basic organization of our messages and the language that helps convey it.

In the Focus on Language section, we looked at 'will' and 'would,' the language of probability, and contrast and comparison.

1) Do you think you have a problem deciding when to use 'will' and 'would'?
2) How can you alert yourself to the possible misuse of 'would'?
3) When will you use the language of probability?
4) When will you use the language of contrast and comparison?

In Focus on Writing, we looked at ways to organize contrast and comparison.

1) How many ways can you think of to organize a message?
2) What are the factors that would make you choose one method over another?

3) Why do we need to organize our messages before we write or speak them?

In Focus on Speaking, we engaged in two group activities: one of evaluation and the other of design.

1) Was the topic of interest to you?
2) Why or why not?
3) What is the purpose of activities like this?
4) Do you like the chance to choose the topic of your group discussions?
5) Why is having this choice important?

chapter 7

Openings and Closings

 FOCUS ON COMMUNICATION

ACTIVITY: Testing Memory

Find a partner. One of you (Partner A) should have a piece of paper and pen handy and the other (Partner B) should have a list of 30 words and a stopwatch.

Partner B hands the list to Partner A to look at for one minute. Then Partner B retrieves the list. Partner A writes down as many words as possible from the list.

Switch places and use a new list.

Together discuss the following questions:

1) Which words on the list were the easiest to remember?
2) The hardest?
3) Where were the words on the list?
4) Were you surprised?
5) What can this experiment tell us about memory and how people notice things?
6) If you were advertising something, where/when would you introduce the name of your product?
7) Why?

ACTIVITY: Writing Up the Experiment (Portfolio Assignment)

Write a memo to your boss describing this experiment and telling the boss what it can teach about positioning in advertisements, letters, memos, presentations, and so on. You may want to look for more information about Serial Position Effect on the Internet or in an encyclopedia.

Serial Position Effect

The brief experiment in the previous activity is a graphic example of two effects on memory: the **primacy effect** and the **recency effect**. We remember the words at the beginning of the list because we rehearse them for recall—the primacy effect. We remember the words at the end of this list because they are the most recently seen words—the recency effect.

The implications for persuasive writing and speaking are important for getting our message across. A good beginning that impresses the audience will mean they will remember what we say first and a good ending will emphasize the idea, action, or conclusion. If the beginning and end of our messages are not clear and convincing, we have wasted a golden opportunity to persuade our audience of the imperative of the message.

 FOCUS ON LANGUAGE

Choosing the right word or phrase is important for both understanding and clarity. We can persuade our audience through logic, but we must never forget the emotional content of what we say. Negative words or words that carry negative or undesirable connotations are usually to be avoided.

In this chapter we will learn how to use the dictionary to help us choose the right word.

ACTIVITY: Using the Dictionary

Look up the following words in your dictionary: innovate, ideal, alternate, specialize, determine, promote, depend, manipulate, reliable, talent, excess.

Other than the definitions, what else does a dictionary tell you about a word? Make a list below of the information you can find in a dictionary.

1.

2.

3.

4.

5.

6.

7.

8.

9.

10.

ACTIVITY: Exploring a Word

In a group, each person takes one word from the above list and explores all the meanings, forms, origins, etc., listed in your dictionary. Find something new or something that makes the word clearer. Report to your group.

ACTIVITY: Focusing on Frequently Confused Words

In your group, divide into two teams. Each team takes one of the pair of the words listed below and looks it up in the dictionary.

- Principal/Principle
- Than/Then
- Who's/Whose
- Personal/Personnel
- Advice/Advise
- Accept/Except
- Affect/Effect
- Beside/Besides
- Choose/Choice
- Among/Between
- Fewer/Less
- Loose/Lose

1) How is the word pronounced?
2) What does it mean?
3) When do you use it?
4) Why do you think you might confuse it with its counterpart?
5) How can you try to remember the difference between them?

ACTIVITY: Finding and Choosing Better Words

In the memo below, find some inappropriate words and grammatical mistakes. With your group, find and correct the errors and choose better words to replace the inappropriate ones.

Memo
To: All Senior Planning Staff
From: Thomas Edwards, VP Office of Corporate Planning
Date: 17 June 2004
Subject: Changes to Annual Corporate Planning Process

Present policy dictates that the annual corporate plan be completed by 1 December. In order to allow more time for externalized document review, the underlined changes have been suggested.

Phase	Item	Present deadline	Proposed deadline
I	Initial department draft	1 September	1 August
II	Revision by Senior Planning Staff	1 October	1 September
III	Presentation of Final Draft to Board of Directors for review	1 November	1 October

These changes would no doubt hit upon your present work procedures, staffing levels, and planning methods. Your comments are now being solicited and manditorily made in writing to this office.

The final deadline is 10 July.

Adapted from Arden and Dowling. 1993. *Business Concepts for English Practice*, p.118.

 FOCUS ON WRITING

Although the following section is about writing, most of the ideas are also applicable to speaking.

Openings

As we have seen by doing the activity in Focus on Communication, the first part of a list, or any communication activity, is better remembered than the middle part. Openings should **capture** our audience's attention, tell them **why** we are communicating, and give them a **roadmap** or **preview** of what the communication will contain. After we have analyzed the audience, decided what the message will be, and how we will send it, we then need to carefully craft our opening. Many writers leave the opening until the last in order to decide exactly what to say. Because the first thing we write or say is so important to our credibility and ultimate success, it is crucial to make our openings very good.

ACTIVITY: Analyzing a Recent Message

Bring to class a recent message you have received.

1) How did it start?
2) What did it contain to capture your attention?
3) Was it effective?
4) Could it have been better?
5) Was the purpose of the communication clear? (Sales message, informational message, etc.)
6) Where was the purpose stated?
7) What kind of language told you the purpose? (For example: 'the purpose of this letter is…')
8) Was there a preview of the contents?
9) How was it done? (Bullet points, list, numbers, general, etc.)
10) Was it adequate in describing what was in the message?

Developing Openings

How to write good openings often confuses and frustrates students. One method is to first decide on the purpose and scope of the communication. Is it a sales letter, an informational memo, or an email requesting action? The purpose, direction, and the tone of the communication need to be decided.

Then we need to decide what will capture our reader's attention. (In the publishing world, this is called 'the **hook**.') When we analyze our audience, we can imagine what they will respond to. It could be something personal (a personal experience), a quotation (from a famous person or a satisfied customer), facts or statistics (about who wants, uses or needs something), a question, a reference to a current event, or a startling statement that is in contrast to our main idea.

The next step is to connect the hook to the purpose in a transition. This can be as simple as a connector such as 'and,' or it can be more complex such as a sentence or two. A good hook will arouse interest, but if readers or listeners do not know why this communication is important or what it hopes to accomplish, they may be confused and lose interest. A preview of the contents, even a short statement such as 'many issues,' will allow the reader or listener to orient themselves on the road map.

Openings contain:

- Hook
- Purpose
- Preview

Closings

As we saw when doing the Serial Position Effect activity at the beginning of this chapter, the last thing we see or hear is remembered better than anything that comes before. This is especially true in speaking where the listener cannot go back to review on his or her own, but must rely on the presenter.

The closing provides an opportunity to reconnect in a more personal way with the audience by using the opportunity to send a goodwill message. Closings can also be used to reinforce a call for action or clarify the next step needed. The end of the message is a place to give information about who to contact for more information, openings hours, and so on. The closing should not introduce new topics but should only be a summary of what has been written or said in the body of the message.

ACTIVITY: Discussing the Closing

Using your recent message, answer the following questions:

1) What was contained in the closing?
2) How did you feel about it?
3) Was it too long or too short? Just right?
4) Why?
5) Could you suggest ways to make it better?

Developing Closings

Closings need to leave the audience with a firm sense of the purpose of the message and a sense of closure. Strong closings should satisfy the audience and not leave them with questions. Possible strategies include a reference to an example, fact, or statistic from the opening or an important point in the body. Another idea for a closing could be a comment about the future or a call to action. Endings should always strive to maintain goodwill with the audience, so an ending that cements this emotional tie with the reader/listener is important. Remember, just as we always need to say a 'goodbye' before we end a conversation, we need to do the same with a written communication.

Closings contain:

- Reference(s) to the message
- Call for action or reference to the future
- Goodwill statement

ACTIVITY: Analyzing and Rewriting

Look at the memo from Thomas Edwards.
1) Is the opening adequate?
2) Does it capture your attention?
3) Does it tell you the purpose?
4) Does it give you a roadmap?
5) Is the closing adequate?
6) Does it summarize the message?
7) Does it call for action?
8) Does it contain goodwill?
9) Can you write a better closing?

ACTIVITY: Writing an Essay on Ethics (Portfolio Assignment)

See the Focus on Speaking activity, Discussing Business Ethics. Write an argumentative essay on one of the ethics scenarios given.

PERSUASIVE WRITING & SPEAKING

 **FOCUS ON SPEAKING**

Openings and closings are at least as important, if not more so, in speaking as in writing. In a business presentation, the audience has little time to waste on long-winded or confusing openings. If we have only 30 seconds to get our message across in an advertisement, our opening is crucial in capturing the attention of our audience. Our closing must leave our audience with good impressions about the message, the sender, and the company or institution we represent, even if the message is not a particularly good one.

ACTIVITY: Presenting Advertisements for the Marketing Exercise

Each group presents the advertisement for their product. Another group evaluates the advertisement. Using the Speaking Evaluation Checklist from Chapter 4, comment especially on the opening and closing of the advertisement.

Creating Arguments

As we saw in Chapter 6, creating a convincing argument demands preparation. A claim should be clear and precise; the support should be relevant, convincing and specific.

ACTIVITY: Discussing Business Ethics

Using one of the scenarios below, work in your group to make good arguments for or against the situation.

1) Discuss the topic in a general way
2) Make notes and categorize them, using criteria/categories
3) Decide on a series of claims
4) Decide what support is needed
5) Prioritize by importance

Business Ethics

Scenario 1
On a business trip to a developing country, you see an interesting and unusual product that you are sure could be successfully marketed in your own country at a price both attractive to the consumer and profitable to you. When you visit the factory that makes this product, you find that the working conditions of the workforce are bad and the pay rates are low.

Should you make a contract with them?

Scenario 2
You are a law officer investigating a case of bribery. During your investigation you find that a few years ago, one of the suspects was very friendly with your son. Your son has recently set up his own business and it is developing well. You are told that if the suspect is put on trial, whether by you or anyone else, your son's business will be ruined and he will never be able to have his own business again.

What could you do and what would you decide to do?

Scenario 3
Your overseas business has been going through a bad period, but recently you have been negotiating for a long-term and valuable contract. At the last meeting, you were taken aside and told that the contract would be signed if you were prepared to make a payment into a numbered Swiss bank account operated by the chief negotiator on the other side.

What would you do?

Scenario 4
Two months ago, your overseas company took over a competitor who had a few months earlier re-equipped its factory with up-to-date machinery. At the time of the takeover, you gave assurances to the workforce that there would be no job losses. Since the takeover, you have tried unsuccessfully to raise finance for similar new machines in your original factory where you have a militant trade union. The easiest solution to the problem is to lay off

the workforce in the recently acquired factory and transfer the machines to your own factory.

1. What problems would you face if you did this?
2. What action would be best and why?

Adapted from Mawer. 1992. *Business Games*. pp.57–58.

FOCUS ON REFLECTION

This chapter introduced the importance of openings and closings. It started with an interactive activity designed to teach Serial Position Effect. These kinds of hands-on activities are designed to teach concepts by engaging students in **discovering** the concept, rather than just being **told** the concept.

1) Do you like these interactive games?
2) How useful do you think they are?
3) What is the importance of discussion after the activity is finished (the debriefing phase)?
4) Do these activities make you curious to read or research more about the topic?

In the Focus on Language, we used our dictionaries.

1) On a scale of 1 to 10 (with 1 being least important), rate how important the dictionary was to you before you joined this class.
2) Has this importance changed?
3) State one important thing you have discovered about the value of a dictionary.

In Focus on Writing, we continued with openings and closings.

1) In this chapter, what have you learned about openings that you will put to use in the near future?
2) What about closings?
3) Are you convinced that openings and closings are important?
4) How important?

In Focus on Speaking, we talked about ethics.

1) How important are business ethics to you as a student?
2) Is it interesting to talk/argue about ethics?
3) Why?
4) How valuable is this kind of 'talk' in helping you develop skills as a 'persuader'?

chapter 8

Formatting the Message

 FOCUS ON COMMUNICATION

The image we project—whether it is in the format and style of our writing, the clothes we wear, or how our voice sounds—affects our **credibility**. Credibility is the authority and trust that receivers see in the sender of the message.

Credibility in writing starts with the format of our written work, which includes the use of space on a page, choice of font and font size, and length of the message. Organizers such as numbers, bullet points, and headings make our work more credible as our audience will trust us to be comprehensible and comprehensive. The opening of a document, where we build common ground and introduce the topic, is especially important. (Remember Serial Position Effect.) Research has shown that the relationship of perceived credibility and persuasiveness is very strong.

Similarly, first impressions count when we meet someone. We have all had the feeling at one time of, "I knew I couldn't trust him from the moment I laid eyes on him!" The formality or informality of our clothes, hair style, jewelry, stance, handshake, and so on, creates impressions on our subconscious.

Body language is said to be responsible for 50–90% (depending on which study we read) of the message in verbal communications. Eye contact, lively gestures, a confident stance, and a pleasant facial expression lend us credibility. We can tell whether someone is smiling only because they think they should or if the smile is from the heart. (Look at the eyes!) A genuine smile is a powerful tool in building credibility.

The confidence that our readers/listeners place in us means that they will pay attention to our message, so building credibility with our audience is crucial to our effectiveness.

Another factor in credibility is choosing the right **channel for communication**. There are some channels of communication that are 'richer' than others. Rich communication is a continuum from text only (the least rich) to a multiple method of text, pictures, voice, and body language (the richest). Some situations such as communicating bad news demand a rich communication channel, otherwise the sender is perceived as being cold and distant. Other situations, such as communicating legal requirements, demand precision, so writing is better, although it is not as rich a channel. Choosing whether to have an individual face-to-face meeting, have a group meeting, write a personal email, send a general memo, or attach a flyer to a common bulletin board, is crucial to our credibility.

Email, having become a very common method of communication in the business world today, is often used in lieu of telephone calls, memos, and letters. But, because it is text only, it is not a rich channel. Emoticons (:)) have evolved to add richness to the message. However, they are frowned upon in the business world as not being professional. So we must decide whether an email, which is quick and can be informal, really is a substitute for phone calls or face-to-face meetings.

 FOCUS ON LANGUAGE

Parts of Speech

Some words can be nouns or verbs, and a different form may be an adjective or an adverb. Some languages can use exactly the same form for each of these functions, but in English, we usually have different forms. These can be confusing.

Finance

- Verb: finance (finances, financing, financed) – to provide money
- Noun: finance (finances) – the activity of providing and managing money, the amount of money a person has
- Adjective: financial – relating to money
- Adverb: financially – relating to money
- Noun: financier (financiers) – a person or company that provides money

Acquire

- Verb: acquire (acquires, acquiring, acquired) – to buy or obtain
- Noun: acquisition (acquisitions) – to make an acquisition is to buy something
- Noun: acquirer (acquirers) – a company or person who buys another company
- Adjective: acquisitive – concerned with getting new possessions
- Noun: acquisitiveness – the quality of being concerned with getting new possessions

Choosing the Right Word

Written language is used in many situations such as in a court of law, in a university textbook, in an advertising brochure, or on a sign in a public place. A formal word used in court may not be appropriate for an advertising brochure. There is a continuum of language from formal to informal and we need to choose a word that fits the social situation.

ACTIVITY: Choosing Formal or Informal

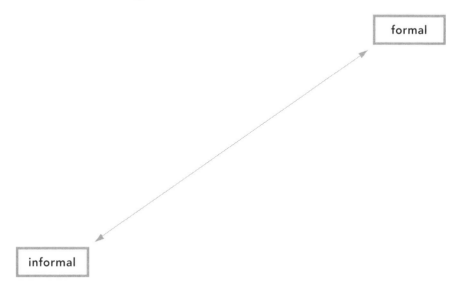

In a group, place the following sets of words on the continuum above:

Set 1
- Periodically
- Regularly
- Every time

Set 2
- Superb
- Amazing
- Cool
- Really good
- Awesome
- High quality
- Bad
- Excellent

When you have done so, answer the following questions:

1) Did everyone agree on where each word should go on the continuum?
2) Does the meaning of words ever change?
3) How important is it to choose the proper formality or informality?

Negative Words

How do we feel when we hear someone tell us, "NO!"? Even though we may be expecting it or it does not really matter very much, we usually do not feel good about it. And we sometimes then feel negative about the sender. How can we keep our audience from feeling angry and hurt, and pay attention to our message? How can we send negative messages and still make our audience believe what we say?

One way is to change our negative words into positive ones. Another way is to soften the negative 'feeling' of a word by choosing another word that carries fewer negative connotations.

Negative to positive

You have failed to complete the project on time.

Better: The project is not finished yet and we need the results now.

Still better: The project should be finished as soon as you can as we are counting on it.

Some words or phrases carry **hidden negatives**. On the surface, there is no negative word or phrase, but if we read and think carefully, we may find that the meaning or connotations are not the tone we want to convey:

Please be patient as we upgrade your building's air-conditioning system. (The hidden message is that there will be problems!)

Better: Upgrading the air-conditioning system will take at least six weeks. Please call us if you have any questions.

Still better: When the new upgraded air-conditioning system is in place six weeks from now, we can all enjoy clean, cool air from a quiet system.

Countable, Uncountable, and Collective Nouns

Countable nouns have singular and plural forms. Uncountable nouns have only one form. Collective nouns are either singular or plural depending on the context.

The determiners 'few' and 'many' are used with countable nouns; 'less' and 'much' are used with uncountable nouns:

Few companies, many computers

Less time, much energy

Subject-verb agreement can be difficult with collective nouns because we must decide first of all, if the subject is acting as a whole (singular) or as individual members (plural), as seen in Chapter 3:

The committee (as a whole) agrees on the budget.

The committee (as individuals) are compiling lists of potential donors.

Consistency

Shifts in verb tense, mood, or person cause confusion in our readers. We have already seen that verb tense shifts can be confusing, and mood shifts are similar. Maintaining a consistent point of view in person and number lends clarity and credibility to our message:

> If you are a person looking for a job, you should have a solid CV. (You-you)

> If a person is looking for a job, he or she should have a solid CV. (Person – he/she, both are third-person singular)

> If a person is looking for a job, you should have a solid CV. (Shift in point of view from third-person singular to you)

Collective nouns can give us trouble in this case, as we must first determine whether the collective is acting as a unit or as individuals:

> The staff is counting on Roger to prepare its report. (Singular)

Pronoun Reference

As we can see from the above example, the pronoun 'its' refers to the staff, which is singular in this case. This is an example of pronoun reference. Correct choice of pronouns adds to clarity and understanding, just as ambiguous, unclear, or distant pronouns can cause confusion:

> Jane pointed out to Hwee Hoon that since her cat was shedding, she had cat hair all over her new suit she was wearing for the job interview. (This sentence is confusing because we are not sure who owns the cat, who has cat hair on her suit, and who has the job interview.)

> The student found himself unanimously elected president of a group of rap music lovers who was not affiliated. ('Who' refers to 'student', but 'who' is far removed from 'student'.)

Adapted from Glenn, Miller, Webb, and Gray. 2004. *Hodges' Harbrace Handbook*, p.356.

ACTIVITY: Rewriting for Clarity

As a group, rewrite the two example sentences above to make them clearer.

ACTIVITY: Finding and Correcting the Errors

In the following email, find some inappropriate words and grammatical mistakes with your group. Correct the errors and choose better words.

Formatting the Message

To: Application@bilin.com
Cc:
Subject: Documentation and Training Team Leader
Attach: Sujata Nathan CV.doc

Hello!

After reading your posting on the STC job board, I knew I had to submit my CV. I have been considering a chance since receive my masters degree a few months ago. The job you posted resonated close with many goals I have founded for myself.

I am a motivate and experienced technical writer with over ten years experiences. For the past four years, I have worked for a consulting company creating documentation and training materials for a variety of companies and industries, developing a broad range of writing knowledge. I have led a number of project development teams and I know how to motivate other writers and trainers. I develop documentation and training sets for both internal and external training audiences, determined schedules, and managed training facilities for not a few clients.

I am looking for a position with a fast-growing company. I enjoy the change and challenge that are part of the Internet experience. I am looking forward to discussing my qualifications with you. Bilin Company can contact me at the above email address or they can use the phone numbers listed on my CV.

Sincerely,

Sujata Nathan

Adapted from Goodall and Goodall. 2002. *Communicating in Professional Contexts*, p.225.

After your group has found and corrected all the errors, assess your own mistakes.

1) Which errors did you not catch?
2) Why?
3) Which ones were easy for you?
4) Which ones were difficult?

As a group, make a list of the most frequent errors you and your team mates have made.

 FOCUS ON WRITING

ACTIVITY: Analyzing Email

With your group, discuss the following questions about the email from Sujata Nathan:

1) Who is the audience?
2) What is the purpose?
3) What is in the introduction?
4) Is it sufficient?
5) How is the body organized?
6) What is the closing?
7) Is email the right channel to use in sending this message?
8) What other channel could be used?

 FOCUS ON SPEAKING

Debate

Debating in a formal way is not often done outside the classroom, but as a process of stating and defending an opinion, it is an excellent way to make us better at persuasion. Being a good debater means that we must clearly state our claims and give explanations and examples that support our claims. It is not important whether we personally believe the side that we argue for, but how well we put our arguments. We must also consider our opponents' point of view and think of what they will use as support in order to counter their claims. This is similar to how we analyze our audience, so this, too, is useful in sharpening our skills of persuasion. The rebuttal part of the debate tests our ability to think on our feet.

ACTIVITY: Preparing for your Debate

In a few weeks, everyone will take part in a debate. Below are the steps that must be taken to prepare for the debate. This is followed by a description of the way to conduct the debate. Finally, there are guidelines for evaluating the debaters.

Preparation

1. Form teams of 6–8 students.
2. Decide on a proposition that will be in the form of a statement.
3. Divide into two even sides: For and Against. Each side meets separately to plan its strategy. Each member must prepare a part of the argument. If there are three team members, one should deliver the opening statement and preview the points to be made. The second person elaborates on the points, giving specific examples and bolstering the argument with authoritative sources. The last person sums up and goes over the points, perhaps relating the topic to the audience personally in order to gain their emotional sympathy. Remember to think of your opponents' arguments as well as your own, so that you can make a good rebuttal.
4. Each member rehearses his or her formal presentation.

The debate

1. Each side presents its arguments alternately, beginning with the 'For' side. That is, For Speaker 1 presents, then Against Speaker 1, then For Speaker 2, and so on. Each speaker stands to present his/her case and has three minutes to present.
2. After all the speakers have presented their arguments, there will be a 15-minute 'Free Rebuttal' session. The first speaker will be a volunteer from the For side. Each volunteer speaker has only one minute to speak, ask a question, or answer a question. No one may interrupt another speaker. To indicate a willingness to speak or ask a question, the speaker must stand. No speaker may take two 'turns' in a row. A good debater is one who valiantly defends his/her position by being willing to speak and ask questions. At the same time, a debater must be polite, must not interrupt other speakers, or use offensive language to make a point.

PERSUASIVE WRITING & SPEAKING

Determining the winner
The criteria will be based on the following:

- Speakers' presentation skills
- Clarity of arguments
- Willingness to speak during the rebuttal period
- Politeness and fair play

ACTIVITY: Discussing Business Ethics

Using one of the four scenarios below, work in your group to make good arguments for or against the situation.

1) Discuss the topic in a general way
2) Make notes and categorize them, using criteria/categories
3) Decide on a series of claims
4) Decide what support is needed
5) Prioritize by importance

Business Ethics

Scenario 1
Nadia was a single mother with young school-going children. She worked full-time for her company and often stayed late to work overtime. She had promised to take her children shopping for school supplies but usually found herself too tired with too many things to do. Nadia noticed the variety of office supplies in the supply room and realized that her children would find some of them quite helpful in completing their school projects. Especially of interest to her were the marker pens, cards, and glue.

One evening when she was working late and no one else was in the office, she took several marker pens, a couple of sticks of glue, and a stack of cards. Her children were delighted with the supplies and put them to immediate use. Nadia had mixed feelings. She felt guilty about 'stealing' the office supplies, but she was pleased with the satisfaction it brought her children. She rationalized that since she was a valuable employee and willing to work overtime whenever necessary, she deserved them.

Scenario 2
Abdul worked as an administrative assistant to a regional sales manager of a large appliance company. His manager traveled extensively but

communicated with him a great deal via email and telephone. Abdul was used to working independently, and he enjoyed the job. He was taking a Web design class at the local community center. Sometimes during slow periods at work, he would use the computer to do his homework. He did not think this was a problem since he always finished his job responsibilities first.

While on a business trip, Abdul's manager called, asking him to look on her computer for a specific file. While searching for it, Abdul came across some Web history of pornographic sites. He was stunned. He worried about it but eventually decided not to say anything to his manager since both of them were using company computers for personal use.

Scenario 3

Asako was fairly new as the administrative assistant to Maria, who was supervisor of the accounts receivable department. Asako noticed that Betty, a book-keeper, spent a lot of time in Maria's office. This seemed odd since her job responsibilities did not require her to spend that much time with Maria.

In the canteen, Asako learned through the grapevine that Betty was the company 'snoop' and was notorious for spreading vicious and often incorrect gossip. Asako was disappointed that Maria seemed to appreciate the gossip Betty was telling her. Did it empower Maria to know all the dirt about people? Asako wondered if Maria was able to sort out the truth from the dirt. Of what benefit was this gossip to Maria? Asako wondered what she should or could do.

Scenario 4

Omar was shown a copy of a well-prepared report that was presented to the executive board at the university where he worked. The person showing it to him thought he might like to review it since it dealt with the campus where he worked. It had an attractive cover, so he opened it immediately. Omar's response was one of shock. It was the report he had developed six months earlier, word for word. Even the formatting of the document was the same. Someone had deleted his name at the end of the report and added another one. Omar was furious.

Adapted from Bennett. 2003. *Ethics in Business*, pp.79–85.

FOCUS ON REFLECTION

In the Focus on Language section, we concentrated on finding the right word and consistency.

1) Why is word choice important?
2) Why should we care whether we use men/boys or women/girls?
3) What can be the result of using negative language?
4) How well do you control your pronoun references?
5) How can you improve?

In Focus on Writing, we again looked at the topic of analyzing and evaluating.

1) Have your ideas changed about the value of analysis and evaluation through this course?
2) How?
3) Why?

In Focus on Speaking, we began the preparation for our debates and the reasons why we are doing this exercise.

1) Do you prefer doing 'fun' activities in class such as debates or do you prefer working on 'real' messages such as reports?
2) Why?
3) What is the value of each?

chapter 9

Editing and Evaluation

 FOCUS ON COMMUNICATION

Revising and **editing** our work means to make sure everything is as good as we can make it before sending it to our audience. Just as we look into the mirror before we go to work or to class in the morning to make sure our hair is combed and our attire is neat, we must make sure our work is polished.

Revising our work is similar to reflection. We need to ask ourselves the fundamental questions of: who our audience is, what our purpose is, and how the communication looks (the format). This can be considered the forest. Editing for organization, layout, sentence structure, consistency, choice of words, and grammar is like looking at the individual trees that make up the forest. Both are important.

In this chapter, we will look at ways to help us edit our work. We have reviewed many grammar points and have practiced finding and correcting these errors. But it always seems easier to find someone else's mistakes than our own. If we have identified the weak areas in our writing or speaking, we can begin to find ways to identify and correct them.

 FOCUS ON LANGUAGE

Gerunds and Participles

Verb forms that are used as nouns or adjectives are called verbals. Because they started out as verbs, verbals can have objects and modifiers. The '...ing' is the ending of both gerunds and participles. A participle is a verbal that acts as an adjective. A gerund is a verbal that acts as a noun, so we find them used as subjects and objects:

Planning her questions carefully, she was able to hold fast-paced and engaging interviews. (The participle 'planning' describes how she was able to do something)

The reporter providing the most accurate account of the stock market plunge was once a broker. (The participial phrase helps distinguish this reporter from the others)

Writing a useful textbook was her only goal. ('Writing' is a gerund that takes an object and functions as the subject of the sentence)

My neighbor enjoys playing the stock market. (The gerund phrase is the object)

Because gerund phrases act as nouns, pronouns can replace them:

That was her only goal. ('That' refers to 'writing')

He enjoys it. ('He' refers to 'neighbor' and 'it' refers to 'playing')

Dangling Participles and Referents

A **dangling modifier** is a word or phrase that does not clearly modify another word or word group in the sentence. **Misplaced modifiers** are words or phrases that are too far from the words they modify and so they can confuse the reader. Note that computer spell-checkers can rarely identify dangling or misplaced modifiers, so we must learn to catch them ourselves.

The meaning of the sentence can change according to the position of the modifier:

The worker who fell had tried to help his friend.

The worker had tried to help his friend who fell.

In this sentence, the dangling phrase has no clear word to which it refers:

Using accounting software, limitations were detected in the audit for last year.

In these sentences, the modifiers are too far from the reference to make sense:

Sitting on my desk for two weeks, I finally finished writing the reports.

She promised to return the library books in her email message.

Flying around in a circle above the tree, I saw the new airplane toy advertised in the flyer.

After spending an hour in the waiting room, the secretary finally told her the boss was not in.

In this sentence, the referent is not clear:

At the age of eight, my family finally bought a computer.

Adapted from Glenn, Miller, Webb, and Gray. 2004. *Hodges' Harbrace Handbook.*

ACTIVITY: Rewriting for Clarity

Rewrite the above sentences to create clear references between phrases and what they modify.

Sentence fragments

A **sentence** is a group of words that has a main subject, a main verb, and expresses a complete thought. If a group of words lacks one of these parts, it is a **fragment**. Fragments can be sentences that have no subject, have no verb, or have a verb form that cannot be a main verb ('…ing' used alone, 'to' before the verb). The most common mistake in sentence fragments is to have a subject and a verb that are preceded by a subordinator:

Gill going to the store room. ('…ing' form used alone)

When Sam gets his monthly pay statement. ('When' is a subordinator. We need more information about Sam and the pay statement to understand the complete thought)

Because the shipment arrived in the warehouse last week. ('Because' is a subordinator and so this is an incomplete thought)

Some of the subordinators that create incomplete thought are: because, although, before, after, even though, how, if, since, that, unless, until, what, when, where, and why. One way to avoid sentence fragments is to identify sentences that begin with the subordinates above and then to read the sentence carefully to make sure that there is a complete thought.

Note that a command is a sentence even though it may have no subject. The 'you' is understood:

(You) Close the door, please.

ACTIVITY: Finding and Correcting the Errors

In the student Professional Attachment e-log below, find and correct the errors.

> **Week 2**
>
> This week, I was assigned to work on the accounts of another company, Nanyang Business Associates. Initially, I thought the task would be similar to how Alpha's accounting records are done. However, accounting records were different and unique for each company in the way they are presented and recorded. As such, the initial phrase of doing Nanyang's accounts was difficult and I had to seek advice and help from my colleagues. ACCPAC was also customized for different clients so that reference to how the past accounting records were done was necessary for consistency. Like Alpha's, I was given three month's accounts to consolidate including a new task which was to do bank reconciliation for Nanyang.
>
> After doing these two assignments, I realized that accounting is basically monotonous but challenging. You have to be a meticulous and careful person to be able to perform the task well. The most difficult task is not to search for the numbers, but to find the set of invoices and records which the companies might have misplaced and asking them for any missing pieces which was troublesome and hard process.
>
> Besides working on Nanyang's accounts, I helped my colleague translate a Chinese financial statement of a Chinese company. My study of Business Chinese as my general elective came in very handy, applying what I had learnt in my work.

Week 3

As the Nanyang accounts were more complicated, I was lengthened to be finished this week before I continued on the accounts of a new company. I learnt that accounting is not simply keying in numbers but understanding the workings of the company alone was crucial to better understand how the cash flows around the company and its clients. Besides being trained to work with the accounting software, ACCPAC, I realized how important a company's culture is to the success of a company. I found out that the culture of the organization is typically created unconsciously, based on the values of the top management or the founders of an organization. Being a small accounting firm, the staffs work closely together and have established a strong bond within the company. As I have worked in other companies before, there is a similarity among the different roles in the companies. Bosses of the companies tend to be most aggressive ones who are there to monitor and in a way "motivate" workers to work more efficiently. Perhaps, this is one way a company can improve and increase its sales through "pushing". A compensation plan might in a way help the company improve its sales.

Within a small company, communication is direct from the boss to his staff. As such, any areas which the staff is unsure of were cleared immediately with the boss. I've also learnt that to lead a company well, a boss should be involved in the workings of every staff within your company to earn the respect of your staff, not just delegate the job to your staff and totally leave the job for them to settle and have a very clear and analytical set of mind to ensure that your staff's queries are answered. Open communication within a company helps the competency and to speed up productivity of work in the company.

After your group has found and corrected all the errors, assess your own mistakes.

1) Which errors did you not catch?
2) Why?
3) Which ones were easy for you?
4) Which ones were difficult?

As a group, make a list of the most frequent errors you and your team mates have made.

FOCUS ON SPEAKING

ACTIVITY: Preparing for your Debate

Within your group, work on coordinating your debate so that there is no discrepancy or overlap. Help one another. Practice.

Learning Strategies

To learn anything, we have to have a method of doing so. Do we listen only? Or do we do an activity to help us learn? If someone tells us something, do we always remember it? What about showing? Learning how to write and speak well means that we have to adopt learning strategies. Knowing how we, as individuals, learn and then capitalize on that knowledge, can help the process.

ACTIVITY: Discussing Learning Strategies

In groups of three or four, discuss your own learning strategies by answering the following questions.

1) Make a list of all the different kinds of learning strategies you can think of; for example, memorizing mathematical formulas, writing notes in class, revising in a group, etc.
2) Which ones were the most successful (a) in the short term and (b) in the long term?
3) Which ones did you enjoy the most? Why?
4) Are you a visual, an aural, or a kinesthetic learner? (Look up these words in the dictionary if you do not know them.)
5) Which strategies match which type of learner?
6) Is there any point in trying to change your learning strategies, or are they fixed in stone?
7) What influences your choices?

FOCUS ON WRITING

Revising means rethinking while editing focuses on smaller tasks. In all the chapters so far, we have found errors in the sample writing. As part of reflection practice, we have looked at the errors we missed. First, we must understand the grammar and what the error is, and then we have to learn to identify it.

Now that we have had many opportunities to find errors in the samples in the book and in our peers' work, we need to move on to concentrate on finding and correcting our **own** mistakes.

Here are some useful hints.

- **Verb tenses:** Underline all verbs in a paragraph. Decide what each tense is and why you used it. To check consistency, look at the first verb in the paragraph. A general rule is to use the same tense throughout the paragraph or passage. However, each sentence or phrase must be judged on the content and the context of that particular sentence.
- **Subject-verb agreement:** Underline all verbs and double underline the subjects. Do not forget double subjects or gerunds used as subjects. Then decide if the subject is singular or plural. Then check the verb for agreement. Remember that the third-person singular is the only verb that will normally give us trouble.
- **Articles:** There are three articles (a, an, the) and the zero article (no article) to worry about. Put a caret (^) in all places where an article might be. Then see if there is an article and which one it is. Then decide if it is the correct article. If there is no article, decide if one is needed. Remember that 'an' is 'a' before a vowel sound, so do not forget adjectives and other words that start with a vowel sound.
- **Will and would:** Underline any use of will and would. Carefully apply the rules of usage for will and would.
- **Word choice and parts of speech:** Underline any word you are unsure of. Check your dictionary for meaning and usage.
- **Sentence fragments, and dangling and misplaced modifiers:** Underline any sentence that begins with a subordinator. Check to see that it contains a subject and a verb and that it expresses a complete thought. Check for modifiers that are phrases and then make sure there is a noun nearby to which the phrase refers.

ACTIVITY: Portfolio Editing

Bring your portfolio to class. Exchange it with your classmate. Practice editing using the rules outlined above. Make note of the errors in your partner's work, for you and your partner.

1) Did you find any errors?
2) How did you find them?
3) What were they?
4) In giving feedback to your partner, were you specific?
5) Did you show your partner where the mistakes were and how you found them?
6) Were you helpful and kind?

FOCUS ON REFLECTION

This chapter focused on editing and how we can use this final wrap-up as a way to make our writing (and speaking) more credible and thus more persuasive.

In Focus on Language, we looked at misplaced modifiers and sentence fragments.

1) Is this an easy topic for you?
2) Why or why not?
3) Is this a problem in your group?

In Focus on Speaking, we prepared for our debate.
1) How important is preparation for a speaking event?
2) Is the preparation for a team different from individual preparation?
3) How?
4) Which would you rather do, individual or team presentations?
5) Why?

In the Focus on Writing segment, we practiced editing using some hints introduced in this chapter.

1) Did these hints help make it easier to spot errors?
2) How important is it to make something look or sound 'perfect'?
3) Why do we ask someone else to take a look at our work before sending or speaking it?
4) How useful is the dictionary?

chapter 10

Putting It All Together

 FOCUS ON COMMUNICATION

Tone refers to the writer's attitude. This includes how the sender of the message feels about the topic, and also about the audience. Tone is conveyed through **word choice** and **sentence structure**.

Word choice can be as simple as choosing the most accurate word that describes the situation, or it can be as complex as looking in the dictionary for connotations. Negative words or words that contain hidden negative connotations, formal as opposed to informal words, and the choice of 'will' or 'would' for requests are some examples of how tone is conveyed through word choice.

Tone can also be seen in structure, both sentence structure as well as organizational structure. Tone can be seen in polite sentence structures; for example, whether we choose to make something a command or a request. The organizational structure of a message can also convey the tone. Being careful to create a buffer or to find common ground at the beginning of a message conveys the attitude of the sender to the receiver.

Closings with well-chosen words and phrases that convey a sense of persuasion, apology, goodwill, or an understanding of the sensitive nature of the message are also examples of organizational structure that convey tone.

Tone in introductions (remember Serial Position Effect) is especially important. How the topic is introduced and what we choose for an 'attention getter' lend credibility to our message. The tone set by the sender has to be selected with an understanding of how the audience will view the purpose and the context. Consistent tone is important for creating and maintaining credibility.

Tone is also linked to cultural appropriateness and power distance. How a culture views the proper social distance measured by terms of respect and deference varies from one culture to another. Misreading the cultural tone can lead to misunderstanding and loss of credibility. An example of this is the Western custom of addressing someone by their given name even if that person is the boss or a superior. The absence of a title and the familiarity of using a given name may present an uncomfortable situation for an Asian. On the other hand, using a full title and surname, while more comfortable for Asians, may make an American feel isolated and set apart.

Understanding how our audience understands the attitude we intend to convey by our tone will make our communications more effective and credible.

 FOCUS ON LANGUAGE

Maintaining consistency is important to tone. Credibility and effectiveness will be lost if there are swings between formal and informal tone or if the message is not culturally sensitive.

ACTIVITY: Finding and Correcting the Errors

In the letter below, underline the grammatical errors and poor word choices that affect tone. Underline them and then in the margin, indicate the correct grammar or another word. Check with your group to make sure you have corrected all the errors.

Nanyang Business Associates

19 October 2004

Yu Xing
Yin Biao Gardens
Pudong, Shanghai
PRC

Dear Mr. Yu,

Get ready for a hot new toy that will drive kids wild with excitements!
Nanyang Business Associates is proud to introduce to you the *Wolverine Off-Road Machine* – the latest and greatest in motor toy technology.

The *Wolverine Off-Road Machine* is an off-road, four-wheel motorized vehicle that offer oodles of fun for children ages seven to twelve. Available in gray with blue stripes, each car proudly carried the Wolverine logo on the side. The car's dimensions are 1.5 meters in length and 1.3 meters in width, providing ample room for two passengers. By including features such as a durable metal frame, a five horsepower engine, and a three liter fuel tank, the *Wolverine Off-Road Machine* has speed ahead of the competition by offering your customers' children the most realistic driving experience possible.

Not only is the *Wolverine Off-Road Machine* fun for the kids, but it is also worry-free for their parents. Due to features such as seat belts, running lights, and helmets (all included with each purchase), your employees can assure your customers of the guaranteed safety of this revolutionary new vehicle. Moreover, because our engineers have included adjustable speed control in the machine's design, allowing parents to monitor and set the speed up to a maximum speed of 25 kilometers per hour.

Your store can be the first to offer this sensational new toy to your area. The *Wolverine Off-Road Machine* sells for a retail price of $500; yet if you buy two or more, you would be able to purchase them for $450 each.

All you have to do is to return the enclosed purchase order form TODAY, indicating the quantity of your order. If you have any questions concern further details about this product, you may contact the following people in the Wolverine Division of Nanyang Business Associates: Gail Teo, Cecil Tan, or Larry Warner.

Allow yourself this opportunity to be the first to market this revivifying new toy in your area. Beat your competition by ordering your shipment of the *Wolverine Off-Road Machine* today!

Sincerely,

James Wong
Director of Marketing and Research

Enclosure

Adapted from Featheringham and Baker. 2001. *Applications in Business Communication*, p.61.

After your group has found and corrected all the errors, assess your own mistakes.

1) Which errors did you not catch?
2) Why?
3) Which ones were easy for you?
4) Which ones were difficult?

As a group, make a list of the most frequent errors you and your team mates have made.

 FOCUS ON WRITING

ACTIVITY: Peer Editing

Take your final portfolio assignment and exchange it with another member of your team. Answer the following questions:

1) What kind of attention-getter did your partner use?
2) Was there a roadmap or preview?
3) How was the body organized?
4) Could a reader write an outline based on this?
5) How many topics were there? Subtopics?
6) Were they clear?
7) Were there examples and explanations (support)?
8) Were they sufficient?
9) Were they clear?
10) What did the conclusion contain?
11) Did it make reference to major points?
12) Was there a call for action or a recommendation?
13) Most importantly, were you, the reader, convinced?
14) Why?
15) Was it due to logos, pathos, or a combination?
16) Locate the key sentences or passages that convinced you (or were meant to, but failed).

Putting It All Together

17) Do you have any suggestions for making a better argument?
18) Did you find any grammatical errors?
19) What were they?
20) How did you spot them?
21) Were you able to explain what was wrong to your team mate?

ACTIVITY: Analyzing a Letter

Take the above letter about the Wolverine Off-Road Machine and answer Questions 1-17.

 FOCUS ON SPEAKING

ACTIVITY: Debating

See Chapter 8 for instructions on how to conduct your debate.

Your teacher will be looking for how well you deliver your presentation as well as how well you structure and organize your speech. Participating in the rebuttal session will stretch your speaking proficiency, especially 'speaking on your feet' skills.

ACTIVITY: Deciding the Winner

After the debate, the 'other' debate team decides who won the debate. In a group, discuss the following to help you decide who won:

1) Which side do you think won? (First or gut reaction)
2) Who convinced you?
3) How? (Be specific. For example, 'Speaker 1 pointed out...')
4) Did the speaker use logos or pathos?
5) Which was more powerful in this debate?
6) Why?
7) How well did the 'team' work together? (Be specific.)
8) What feedback would you give the speakers? (Be specific and be kind)
9) How could the losing side win next time?

FOCUS ON REFLECTION

In this chapter, we have tied up the course. Our portfolios are finished and we have demonstrated our argumentative speaking skills. Now is the time to look back on the most memorable moments of the course. By reflecting on what we have done and how it has helped us, we can fix those concepts into our knowledge bases and those skills into our repertoire of competencies. We can congratulate ourselves on becoming more persuasive communicators.

In Focus on Communication, we covered many ideas very briefly.
1) What was the most important concept you learned?
2) How will you use it in your other courses?
3) In a future job?

In Focus on Language, we looked at many grammar points as well as learning how to use the dictionary.

1) Without looking back at the text, what was the most important point you learned?
2) Why?
3) Which language concept is still difficult for you?
4) Why?
5) How can you make it easier?
6) Offer suggestions to your team mates.

In Focus on Writing, we reviewed different parts of a communication event, practiced how to organize our writing, and most importantly, how to review what we and our team mates have written.

1) What one idea have you thoroughly learned?
2) Why?
3) How?
4) What idea(s) do you still need to work on?
5) Get your team mates to give you suggestions on how you might achieve your goal.

In Focus on Speaking, we engaged in actual speaking from the first day. The aims of these activities were to make you a more confident speaker, to make you aware of the qualities of a good business presenter, and to learn to evaluate your own and others' speaking skills.

1) Which speaking activity was the most fun?
2) Why?
3) What did you learn from it?
4) What would you advise younger students about speaking skills?

In Focus on Reflection, we thought about what we did, how we felt about it, how useful we thought it was, and thought about plans for change in the future.

1) What do you think was the purpose of this kind of reflective exercise?
2) Did you find it useful?
3) Why or why not?
4) Would you recommend this to other students or teachers?
5) Why or why not?

We have seen that a letter, memo, or speech should have an ending that leaves the receiver with a clear idea of the message and a good feeling about the sender. We hope this last chapter has helped firm up ideas and left us all with a feeling of competency that we can all be persuasive writers and speakers.

bibliography

Arden, M.M. and Dowling, B.T. 1993. *Business Concepts for English Practice*, 2nd ed. Heinle.

Bennett, C. 2003. *Ethics in Business*. South-Western.

Featheringham, R.D. and Baker, B.P. 2001. *Applications in Business Communication: Communicating at GEI*. South-Western.

Glenn, C., Miller, R.K., Webb, S.S., and Gray, L. 2004. *Hodges' Harbrace Handbook*, 15th ed. Wadsworth.

Goodall, H.L. and Goodall, S. 2002. *Communicating in Professional Contexts: Skills, Ethics, and Technologies*. Wadsworth.

Hamilton, C. with Parker, C. 2001. *Communicating for Results: A Guide for Business and the Professions*, 6th ed. Wadsworth.

Mawer, J. 1992. *Business Games*. Heinle.

Wilson, P. and Glazier, T.F. 2004. *The Least You Should Know About English, Form B Writing Skills*, 8th ed. Heinle.

Wingersky, J., Boerner, J., and Holguin-Balogh, D. 2003. *Writing Paragraphs and Essays: Integrating Reading, Writing, and Grammar Skills*, 4th ed. Wadsworth.